Drugs, Food, Sex and *God*

Library and Archives Canada Cataloguing in Publication

Baxter-Holder, George, 1966-, author
    Drugs, food, sex and God : a convicted criminal becomes a doctor through the power of intention / Dr. George Baxter-Holder.

Issued in print and electronic formats.
ISBN 978-1-77141-092-2 (pbk.).--ISBN 978-1-77141-093-9 (html)

    1. Baxter-Holder, George, 1966-. 2. Self-actualization (Psychology). 3. Physicians--United States--Biography.   4. Ex-convicts--United States--
Biography. I. Title.

R154.B39A3 2015   610.92   C2014-906483-7
                                             C2014-906484-5

Drugs, Food, Sex and *God*

An addicted drug dealer
goes from convict to doctor
through the power of intention

Dr. George Baxter-Holder

First Published in Canada 2015 by Influence Publishing

© Copyright Dr. George Baxter-Holder
All rights reserved. No part of this publication may be reproduced, stored in or introduced into a retrieval system, or transmitted, in any form, or by any means (electronic, mechanical, photocopying, recording or otherwise) without the prior written permission of the publisher. This book is sold subject to the condition that it shall not, by way of trade or otherwise, be lent, resold, hired out, or otherwise circulated without the publisher's prior consent in any form of binding or cover other than that in which it is published and without a similar condition including this condition being imposed on the subsequent purchaser.

Narcotics Anonymous World Services, Inc. *Living Clean: The Journey Continues*. Van Nuys, CA: NA World Services, Inc., 2013. Reprinted by permission of NA World Services, Inc. All rights reserved.

Book Cover Design: Jamie Yeung
Editing Team: Susan Kehoe, Nina Shoroplova and Jennifer Kaleta
Typeset: Greg Salisbury
Portrait Photographer: Maurice Labrecque, Maurice Photo Inc.

DISCLAIMER: This book has been created to inform individuals with an interest in taking back control of their own health and life. It is not intended in any way to replace other professional health care or mental health advice, but to support it. Readers of this publication agree that neither Dr. George Baxter-Holder nor his publisher will be held responsible or liable for damages that may be alleged or resulting, directly, or indirectly, from their use of this publication. All external links are provided as a resource only and are not guaranteed to remain active for any length of time. Neither the publisher nor the author can be held accountable for the information provided by, or actions resulting from accessing these resources. All opinions in this book are those of the author.

This book is joyfully and gratefully dedicated to my dear parents, George and Carol Baxter. Without the current of love that is represented by their more than sixty years together, none of this life would have been possible for me.

TESTIMONIALS

"It takes a brave man to slay dragons! But it takes a stronger man to defeat his own demons lurking within. Dr. George is both a demon and dragon slayer of the bravest kind."
Wesley Eure, Author, Actor, and Producer

"Though not all of us have experienced the same traumatic highs and lows chronicled in this book, all of us can relate to Dr. George's story. His story is about finding courage—about letting go of the past, taking charge of the present, and being the architect of one's own future."
Justice Bobbe Bridge, retired, Founding President/CEO of the Center for Children & Youth Justice

"This story is bold, raw, honest, and inspiring. Dr. George has traversed the depths of the human experience, walked through the dark night of the soul, and come out the other side proving that the Spirit is ever victorious. This is a must-read!"
Reverend Mark Anthony Lord, Creator of Pride 2.0, *Author of The Seven Living Words* **and** *Thou Shall* **Not** *Suffer*

"At the center of this book is the main message that whatever obstacle you are faced with and however much you have drifted off course, you can always steer yourself back on track."
Richard Arnold, Star Trek Expert

"Dr. George transforms the excesses and indiscretions of his past into something cathartic and uplifting for all struggling with the metamorphosis from addiction to recovery."
Chris Aguirre, Founder of KLĒN + SŌBR and Creator of the "*Since Right Now*" podcast

"George Baxter-Holder admits early on that this personal memoir isn't a nice, linear story of one's fall and rise with regard to addiction, drugs, and the loss of self. Rather, his tale of addiction reads like rapid, gushing prose—long-suppressed, yet miraculously finding its home on paper. Baxter-Holder's story proves that anyone at any time can do an "about face" and change the seemingly unchangeable. Within these pages you'll find his template for recovery. With the smallest of willingness it can become your template too."
David Ault, Author of *The Grass Is Greener Right Here*

"An honest, raw, and insightful recounting of George's incredible journey out of darkness and toward self-acceptance and inner peace. George provides us with a story of hope and the inspiration needed to never give up."
Kelli Benis, Author of *Shredding the Shame*

"This book is a beautiful example of how someone can turn the pain from their past into fuel for their future. George shows such courage by opening up and sharing some of the darkest and most raw experiences of his life. This is a book you won't want to put down."
Melanie Koulouris Moushigian, Aspiring Writer

"Through stories and deep, personal sharing, Dr. George connects us to the struggles each of us may have with self-limiting beliefs, and provides us a way through and a way out. Hearing the stories of others inspires us and informs our own path out of despair and into the life we really want. I love how Dr. George makes this everyone's story through his bravery and personal commitment to find his way."
Barrie Cohen, Curator, *TEDxSeattle*

"Dr. George writes with humor, finesse, and intelligence. It is so inspiring to see what can blossom in one's life ... to go from meth addict to doctor really says it all!"
Andrea Lane, Singer and Songwriter

"Empowering and inspirational, this book is an offer of hope, an impetus for change with a dose of introspection as guidance. As his story unfolds, you are quickly drawn in by the raw truth and humor with which he brilliantly tells it. Dr. George's life is a testament to the fact that the solutions to our problems really do lie within ourselves."
Lucinda Smith, Life Coach/Energy Transformationalist, Founder of The *UN-Learning Center*, Host and Producer of *Healing Yourself* With Lucinda Smith

"From pain to healing, from addiction to happiness, from imprisonment to freedom—this book shows how one man was able to make the shift toward a better life, and through his story we see reflected a path for us to do the same."
Ester Nicholson, Motivational Speaker/Addiction Specialist, Author of *Soul Recovery: 12 Keys to Healing Addiction ... and 12 Steps for the Rest of Us*

"What a fabulous book. You won't want to put it down. The depth of humanity, the honesty of life, the spirit of who he is and where he's been, and the power of transformation—I was so moved by the honesty and incredible force he has to change his life, make a difference, and show others they can too! If you, or someone you know, is not living up to their potential, this IS the book for them. Honest and inspirational—you have the power to "make it happen." Dr. George shows you how he did and how you can too! A great gift for you, your family, and anyone you know. I was so touched by his honesty and his spirit!"
Rochelle Alhadeff, Co-Host of *Chat with Women* Radio Show

"When you fall in love with the greatness and goodness of the human spirit, your love is unconditional. In this tall, beautiful young man's story, Rod and I recognize his genius, the sweet vulnerability of his spirit, and the brilliance of his future."
Lynda and Rod Pressey, aged seventy-four and eighty-one, Show Performers and Producers, *LP Productions*, Creators of *Victorian Country Christmas*

"A powerful story of overcoming seemingly insurmountable challenges sure to inspire, enlighten, and entertain. Like a phoenix, Dr. George rises from the ashes of his past and creates the life of his dreams using the power of intention."
Jake Dekker, Author of *One Kid at a Time*

"I believe vulnerability is divine strength shining light on our deepest secrets for the purpose of healing. When we expose what is hidden, fear can no longer keep us imprisoned. I admire George's courage as he shares his journey through the darkness and into the vibrant light of forgiveness and love. His story is powerful and the tools George shares will provide a sense of hope and inspiration that anything is possible when you believe that your life matters."
Sue Dumais, Best-Selling Author, Award Winning Speaker, *Heart Led Living* Coach, Intuitive Healer

"George's book was an emotional roller coaster story that emerged from a very dark place to achieve something inspiring. It gave me insight into myself and my addictions, helped me see my gifts, and reevaluate my life choices."
Lynnette L., Recovering Addict

"A rare account of intention, hope, heartfelt and soulful honesty, and "yummy deliciousness" in every page."
Michelle A., Recovering Addict

"This book is a must-read for anyone dealing with addiction, either themselves or through seeing a loved one suffer. For me personally, I desperately tried to help two close family members who struggled with drug addiction, but unfortunately they lost their battles to accidental overdoses that ended their lives. I have seen, from the inside, how out-of-control a person can be when plagued with addiction. In his book, Dr. George shares how he got to the 'other side' in such a raw and emotionally vulnerable way that anybody struggling with addiction will gain something remarkable from reading about his journey and his road to recovery.

"Dr. George has captured a unique process that brings to light the depths and complexity of addiction and recovery. Based on his own life experiences, he outlines nine principles that can be applied to healing any addiction, whether it be to drugs, alcohol, sex, food, codependency, just to name a few. The chapter on G.I.F.T.S. helped me clearly understand that the recovery process is not linear, but rather by integrating the nine steps in one's life, anybody can succeed on the road to recovery and get to the 'other side' of addiction."

Lori G., Recovering Indulge-o-holic

"'I needed a deeper spiritual relationship with something.... For me, food and sex provided all of the spiritual void I required at this point.' Dr. George hits the nail on the head here. Unless we fill our spiritual void, that 'hole in our soul,' with our Higher Power, our program of recovery, fellowship with others just like us, and self-love ... unless we take action to do these things, we WILL find something else, even if it's not our drug of choice. Cross-addictions will inevitably bring us back to our drug of choice, and then to death itself. Dr. George speaks the truth when he says, 'The solution would be for me to deepen my relationship with my higher power.' His book is remarkably and refreshingly honest, forthcoming, touching, humorous, and above all—INSPIRING. Thank you, Dr. George!"

Paige M., A Grateful, Sober Alcoholic

"I laughed (right out loud a couple of times), I cried, I reflected, and I cried again, harder. George shares himself with naked abandonment. Corners of a history that most would keep hidden from public light, George reveals with love, a confidence to be admired, and intention. A MUST-read for those in recovery, considering recovery, or searching for direction. I could relate to so much of his story mirroring my own. Drugs, Food, Sex, and God is intentionally, spirit-stirring."

Lori F., Recovering Addict

"Dr. George provides me—a compulsive overeater who has struggled with shaming and blaming myself my whole life—with a fresh perspective and clear way of seeing myself, my choices, and my actions with self-love and acceptance. In sharing and reflecting on his life and the role food plays in my life ... and most importantly how that role can still change, I am able to go deeper in my own journey as a recovering addict. This book gives me hope and joy that my own healing can evolve and strengthen."

Kelly D., Compulsive Overeater

"The extraordinary power of a book written by one addict for other addicts is evident from the first paragraph. This book can change lives. Using his steps, Dr. George takes 'living with intention' from an intangible concept to a concrete reality. I'm all in—I'm inspired to follow Dr. George on this journey to becoming an irresistible positive force in my own life."

Joanne H., Recovering Addict

"This book is unarguably the definitive read for anyone who struggles to discover his or her path in life. For me as a food addict, it was almost as if I had Dr. George inside my head as he shared his strengths and weaknesses; how his self-awareness emerged through the nine steps. The connection I felt reading this book has given me renewed hope and a new perspective in looking at the G.I.F.T.S. in my life. He is profound, brilliant, funny, and engaging. This is a must-read for everyone!"

Nicolette N., Recovering Food Addict

"I can really relate to a lot of the writing in this book. This book is a reflection of who we were and who we are meant to be; they are not the same. George lays it all out without any abandon; he is open about his addiction and his healing. The most important part for me is the healing. I like how there is so much positivity in this book in the midst of all the insecurity and fear. Everyone, no matter where they have come from, could get something out of this book to make their life better."
Candace, Recovering Addict

"Dr. George has been a positive influence, despite or perhaps due to his very colorful life. I can honestly say that after reading his book, I have found a way of also battling the demons that lurk in the dark corners of my own life. He has come through more trials than most, and yet can still shine a positive light upon all those around him."
Terrie S., Recovering Food and Sex Addict

"Told in a voice that's all-too-familiar, George takes the reader on a journey that's sometimes a roller-coaster and sometimes a carriage ride. It's a story that's vibrant, expressive, graphic, heartfelt, passionate, and above all, honest. I'm left with a deep and profound gratitude for the path I've taken and for the knowledge that people, like George, are here to guide and mentor others through their experience, strength, and hope."
Bill C., Recovering Addict

"I hadn't realized the full extent of Dr. George's story until I read his wonderful book. God bless him for his courage in letting us in on his personal struggles, eventual enlightenment, and healing. To know that, through intention, you can become the person you were truly meant to be is a resounding truth that I endeavor to live myself. Learning to listen to the voice of your higher power, and acting on that wisdom, makes all the difference. This book is so encouraging and helpful. I do believe it will make a difference in your own personal struggles. Enjoy, and be inspired and revived."

Merrillee B., Recovered Foodaholic

"Colorful and insightful—this book is a delicious and meaningful read. As a recovering addict, I was inspired by the level of truth that he found and by the key to Dr. George's transformation. I believe anyone, addict or "normy," will be able to extract powerful lessons and be able to apply these lessons to living life well and getting better on all levels."

Kelly A., Recovering Addict

"I read these pages with great anticipation. I am an addict in recovery with twenty-one years clean. I am a proud member of Narcotics Anonymous and highly recommend it to all addicts. These passages from George show great wisdom and insight into the goals of recovery. His nine step suggestions are very deep and personal ideas he has created during his recovery and are 'on-the-money.' As an adjunct to the twelve steps, this book will give an addict additional tools to use … to give a struggling addict more confidence in himself/herself to stay on the road to recovery. Well done, George."

Tom M., Recovering Addict

ACKNOWLEDGEMENTS

There are many I need to thank for making the writing of my story and the giving of my message to you possible.

First and foremost, I thank my Higher Power, God, who has graciously guided me through the most amazing life in recovery.

The book that you are now holding would not have been possible without the tireless encouragement and support of my dear husband, Travis Don Baxter-Holder. The English language is insufficient to express the vastness of the gratitude that I have for you as an amazing spiritual being. I am eternally grateful to have this walk with you. You will forever be my Everything4Always.

To my dear friend, Bill Krutch, thank you for continuing to be an important figure in my life. Thank you for always being there for me with your emotional support, honest feedback, and beautiful raw wit. You have believed in me through much of the unfolding of my life. I would not be the man I am today had it not been for your influence in my life.

Barrie Berger Cohen, you have taught me what true friendship is all about. You have been a strong presence in my life since we were both very young and, despite all of my trials and tribulations, you remain my oldest friend.

Thank you to my spiritual leader, mentor, and friend, Reverend Charles Hall. You have been my compass back to revealing God within me. Your guidance has offered me the wherewithal to circulate abundance in all areas of my life and my life has grown exponentially for it.

To my family, the Baxters, Foleys, and Georges, thank you for believing in me even when I had given up on myself. You have taught me that family is about Love, without condition or excuse.

I want to give special recognition to the men and women I sponsor and who sponsor me, and to my entire recovery fellowship. You all continue to help me strive to become a better man and live with Integrity.

FOREWORD

In the beginning of Dr. George's book, there is a quote that states, "*Healers are spiritual warriors who have found the courage to defeat the darkness of their own souls.*" What a perfect and appropriate description of this amazing Spiritual Being who rediscovered his wholeness through the darkest night of his own soul. Sometimes that is the only way it can be found—through the darkest night, which then inspires us to do the healing work necessary to rediscover the magnificence that was there all along.

Addiction is when one has become enslaved by his sense of powerlessness. It is when one is in bondage to limiting ideas, thought patterns, and behaviors that are out of alignment with wholeness. George talks not only of addiction to drugs in this powerful book, but how he became enslaved to a false identity of himself, and when we falsely identify ourselves as anything less than divine, perfect, and complete, we are indeed powerless and our lives become unmanageable.

But through the power of intention, we get to rebirth ourselves into a life beyond our wildest imaginings. I love that he talks about how the power of intention can be used destructively or constructively because it is impersonal energy that manifests at the level of the consciousness that directed it. It can be used unconsciously or consciously. It is immutable, constant, and unfailing—so if we're using it anyway, why not use it in a constructive and conscious way that leads us in the direction we truly desire to go?

His rigorous honesty and raw vulnerability are humbling, dynamic, and empowering all at the same time. He exposes himself in a way that we can all relate to—because even though our stories may differ, we have all experienced the same feelings of fear, shame, confusion, resentment, as well as joy, excitement, fulfillment, and peace.

What I love most about his work, however, is that it's not just some "tell all" book about his journey. He has used his pain to be of service to others, as well as his joy and celebration. He has designed his Nine Steps of Intention to take you, the reader from the darkest night of your soul to the triumphant victory of your true worthiness.

Drugs, Food, Sex and God is a provocative book that clearly leads us to the powerful realization that God is in it all, all the time, every time, no exceptions!

Ester Nicholson
Motivational Speaker/Addiction Specialist
Author of *Soul Recovery: 12 Keys to Healing Addiction ... and 12 Steps for the Rest of Us*

CONTENTS

Dedication...III
Testimonials... V
Acknowledgements..XV
Foreword...XVII
Contents...XIX
Preface..XXI

Introduction 1
Chapter 1: Struggle 13
Chapter 2: Surrender 31
Chapter 3: Belief..47
Chapter 4: Understanding Your G.I.F.T.S. 57
Chapter 5: Allowing In Your Dreams................101
Chapter 6: Crafting Your Goals..........................123
Chapter 7: Setting The Plan 137
Chapter 8: Taking Action 155
Chapter 9: Celebration 171
Chapter 10: With Firm Intention.......................185

Afterword..203
Resources 205
Author Biography 207
More About the Author 209

"In the great adventure of my life, I now wake up to who I really am. For the many ways I have been lost, I am now found. For the many ways I have harmed, I am now forgiven. For the many ways I have lied, I now live truth. For the many ways I have self-condemned, I am now whole. I have come home to my heart to find what was always waiting for me: an everlasting love affair."

Reverend Charles Hall
Founding Minister, Genesis Global Spiritual Center

PREFACE

I will never forget the feeling I had when I read *A Million Little Pieces*. Author James Frey had captured the feelings I had had so much of my life in brilliant detail. I watched him when he was on Oprah and was fascinated by the bold, vulnerable way he bared his life story. I also vividly remember how betrayed I felt when he went back on Oprah and humbly apologized for what was then downgraded from memoir to semi-fictional novel. What the heck is "semi-fiction?" Is it the same as "kind of pregnant?" I was flabbergasted and disappointed. I decided then and there that I would tell my story someday even though I was still in early recovery and truly trying to find myself and my way. It was not until I became a doctor that I realized that my story had told itself. I had transitioned from being a happy child to the dark corners of prison. I came out a drug-addicted felon yet through my process, I became a doctor.

Let me make one thing clear, I am not a physician. I am a Doctor of Nursing Practice (DNP). This detail may not be important to any of you but it is important to any MDs who may read this. It is my hope that there are plenty of MDs who will pick this book up and read it. I know a few who could benefit from its lessons. I know more than one who have significant issues with food, sex, and maybe even drugs; I've even worked with a cardiologist who was a daily smoker even after his multiple heart stents. Incidentally, he is the only person on the planet who I would insist call me Dr. Baxter-Holder, full name with title. He may not know why but it is about ego, his not mine. For me, I am happy being George or for fun Dr. George. I have really grown quite fond of it and love when patients call me that because it always brings a smile to my face.

There are so many abundant reasons why being called Dr. George makes me smile. The biggest reason is that for the first time in my life I am living up to my potential. It is through the power of intention and living on purpose that I thrive. If those patients and friends knew the horrors I have been through, put myself through actually, they might just … Well I don't know what they might just do but I am willing to find out. Through this process of telling my story, I am willing to be vulnerable and bare some of my innermost secrets. My purpose for doing this is to help people. Even if just one person is saved from having to go through what I have, this project will be worth it. Just one person! As I prepare to share this story, I feel the need for warnings and disclaimers. Humor me. When I say I am going to be vulnerable, I mean in a way that is clear, true, and naked. Many who write about their experiences with addiction and recovery are vague and obtuse. This book has "Drugs" and "Sex" in the title. If the topics of drugs or sex make you squeamish, you might be just a bit uncomfortable. If you are reading this book, you might just want or need to be a little uncomfortable.

I offer you this: I will be as delicate as I can be and leave as much to the imagination as possible. I will use graphic detail only when necessary and will always try to warn my sensitive readers first. Rest assured there will always be a point to the story and that point will always be about intention.

I will not make the same disclaimers about my use of the word "God" nor of the concept of a Universal Spirit. I am profoundly spiritual and have no specific dogma that I follow. There are, however, quotes from various recovery texts contained within this book. I would like to thank the programs of Narcotics Anonymous and Alcoholics Anonymous for offering many people a way to navigate the path back from death. My membership in my own program of recovery is profoundly personal and by no means is this book meant to endorse or seek endorsement of any program.

Last but not least, remember this is my truth, start to finish. There are places where the story may flare dramatic a little, because I tend to be theatrical and dramatic. I am gay after all! The stories are all true, even if they are from my perspective only. I've changed some names when necessary to protect no one in particular. This is a fun and exciting account and I know that if nothing else there will be great entertainment and laughs. My hope is that the nine lessons of living with intention can help with any area of your life where you struggle and are aware that something greater is right around the corner.

Enjoy,
Dr. George

INTRODUCTION

"Healers are Spiritual Warriors who have found the courage to defeat the darkness of their souls. Awakening and rising from the depths of their deepest fears, like a Phoenix rising from the ashes. Reborn with a wisdom and strength that creates a light that shines bright enough to help, encourage, and inspire others out of their own darkness."
Melanie Koulouris

Why did I write this book? This is a very good question with a very long answer. I will try to keep it as brief as I can. First of all, I had to write this book. Not in some freakishly compelling way that I think I have some or all of the answers that you need to live your life. But that I found, in the most miraculous way, some of the answers that I needed to live my own life. As my head began to clear from the fog that my life had become I realized that I had some very simple truths about my life. My life had been a straight line. I could see how I got to this point doing this very thing and I knew that what I was doing was intentional. Think of a key with all of its seemingly erratic shapes, yet the moment you put it in the right lock, the tumblers all fall exactly into place. The key to life is just like this.

I had a very difficult time reconciling that my addiction, which manifested in the use of drugs, overeating, and sex, was just as intentional as my getting clean, going to school, and creating a truly wonderful life for myself. I slowly started to pull apart the aspects of each point in my life that I would have labeled "life struggles" and realized that each had some similar characteristics and patterns.

I was drawn to Wayne Dyer's book, *The Power of Intention*. He defines intention as "a field of energy that flows invisibly beyond the reach of our normal, everyday habitual patterns. It's there even before our actual conception. We have the means to attract this energy to us and experience life in an exciting new way."

These words gave me three distinct ideas about intention and I knew that all of my life was guided by this power—the positive experiences and the negative. Dyer says that it is a field of invisible energy like electricity or gravity, intention is at work irrespective of age, race, sexual identity, or religion. Intention just IS and IS without judgment. It is beyond the reach of our normal, everyday habits, and outside of that which gets labeled "bad" or "good." The second aspect of intention is that it is always there. It does not turn off and on like a faucet but is a steady flow like wind or a river. Finally, intention is attracted to us by our own relationship with it and through it we experience all of life.

I began to explore what steps I could define as a means to attract this energy into my life. This is when I developed my Nine Steps of Living with Intention. I have called them steps because of my personal relationship with the Twelve Step recovery program. These are not those steps. Those twelve steps helped me to get my life back from the darkness of addiction and separation from life itself. If you find yourself in that dark and dismal place, know that you are not alone and that there is a way out from the dark nights of the soul.

Introduction

For those of you seeking to heal addiction, I do recommend Twelve Step recovery and although I have membership in one, and only one, anonymous group I strongly recommend you find one that speaks to you and your needs. I also strongly recommend my friend Ester Nicholson's book *Soul Recovery: 12 Keys to Healing Addiction*. In Ester's powerful book, she uses her own story to guide you to discover your own greatness and power that is within you and help you to heal the unworthiness and poisonous stories of separation, limitation, and lack.

Drugs, Food, Sex and God is my story but not my story through the Twelve Steps; much of the story that follows happened before I even identified that I had a problem that could be addressed by those steps. There were other forces at work in my life. I had potential. I was told that I could be or do anything that I wanted. I had "the means to attract this energy … and experience life in an exciting new way." I did not realize that when I was putting a syringe full of methamphetamines into my veins that I was using the means and attracting this energy. I thought I was just getting high. I also thought that the only person I was hurting was myself, one of the biggest lies an addicted person tells themselves.

This story is not told in a linear fashion. If you are looking for a nice neat historical account of the rise and fall and rise of a meth addict I am sorry to disappoint you. There is nothing neat and linear about drug addiction. The life story of an addict, any addict, is rife with ebbs and flow and eddies that get you and keep you tossing and turning until you make a change. Instead, this story is about the steps it takes to make that change.

Again, I keep using the word "steps" but let me clear that up. "Steps" make it sound so neat and linear but saying "messy pie slices" is not very elegant in a literary way. So, I will use one word when really I am referring to the other. If you take a circle, and cut it in half, half again, and half again, like you would a pie, you are left essentially with eight equal pieces. But I said there were nine "messy pie slices." Oh, crap. Same thing happens when you plan dessert for eight and nine show up, split one in half. On one side of the split piece is where this process starts—Struggle; and on the other is where the process ends—Celebration. It is in the times of Celebration that you realize there is yet another struggle waiting for your attention.

Consider the college graduate all fluffed and puffed in the graduation regalia. There is a buzz and excitement during this celebration time. There are parties, presents, cards, relatives, plans, hopes, and dreams but back in the small dark corner stands a budding struggle; what will I do with the rest of my life? How about the wedding day? It can be the happiest day of a person's life; I know it was mine. Yet, there is a slight tug of "now what" that lurks in the shadows.

One last great example that I have yet to know anything about and don't really want to: the birth of a child. The joy, the tears, the exultation of new life in the world but … who gets up at 3:00 a.m.? where are they going to kindergarten? will they get into private Montessori school? will they get

Introduction

beat up in high school? ... and so it goes. These questions can make new parents more sleep deprived than their bundle of joy! Each wonderful celebration in life leads to new questions and new struggles. Each struggle will ultimately lead to some resolution or celebration. This book helps the reader circumnavigate the messy pie slices.

Each chapter has a step (or slice) at its very core and I open up about my individual story to illustrate how I conquered each slice in terms of some very dark struggles with sexuality, addiction, drug dealing, prostitution, and obesity. It is important that I also share the bright side of my life having come out the other side, and discuss the struggles around getting clean, finding a career, becoming a Doctor Nurse, and falling madly in love and marrying the man of my dreams.

Step One and Step Nine share one slice of the pie—Struggle and Celebration, but the other seven steps are where exploration and joy come alive.

Step Two is about Surrender. It is not about giving up or giving in necessarily but it is about coming over to the winning side. In my life, there were huge surrenders that happened early in life regarding sexuality and addiction. In every life, there are big and small surrenders just like there are big and small struggles. I will never forget the surrender that happened just about writing this book. One day, I opened my journal and I wrote one line that catapulted me in the direction of my dreams. I have been constantly reminded by Henry David Thoreau that, "if one advances confidently in the direction of his dreams ... he will meet

5

with success unexpected in common hours." I am sure that the line I wrote was much more like Snoopy writing, "It was a dark and stormy night." It was not the content of the writing but the energy of the surrender. I stopped fighting myself about it and just laid down the proverbial sword.

Step Three is about Belief. Actually, it is about three different levels of belief, each harder to fully accept than the next. Coming to believe in a Universal power that is everywhere present is usually relatively easy for many people. It was for me. I did not need to look very far to see evidence that a power like that exists. As a young boy, I would stare at the water in Long Island Sound and wonder how it always knew to come back to the same place with every tide, Universal power. I was able to believe in others; parents, friends, community, but there were times when I felt like my belief wavered. The friend who stopped being a friend and I didn't know why, or the community government decided to close a school where my friend's children studied. I remember when I was younger; my mother would make sure I knew where she was going in case "I needed anything." She was not clear that it was for emergencies only, so I had her paged in the grocery store to bring home ice cream. Needless to say, it was not the ice that got creamed. Each particular circumstance went up against my beliefs but overall I still was able to "believe" in others. The hardest thing to do is to believe in myself. It takes constant work and continued vigilance. It takes more than just lip service but takes a commitment to change. When I was young and just starting to experiment with

Introduction

drugs, I had a belief that I was invincible, which was only made stronger by the drugs. When the drugs were gone and I was left with a vacuous void of insecurity and remorse, believing in myself was futile. I had no proof, no data, and no experience on which to base my belief. I had to slowly and intentionally build that belief back up. It still takes constant work and continued vigilance. Left alone with my thoughts I still create only two kinds of movies—horror and science fiction. Coming to believe in myself is learning how to create a love story.

There is a natural flow from creating a love story about yourself to taking stock in everything that makes you uniquely you. Step Four is about Understanding your G.I.F.T.S. Truly taking a deep inventory of the things that make you Grateful; Insecure; things which are your Foundational values; things and situations that Threaten your progress; and what is at your Spiritual center. Having an understanding of all these G.I.F.T.S will reduce the times where your life is just controlled by "I" and "T." I don't know how many times I just acted out of fear and self-loathing because I had no idea just how talented I really was. I remember one time in the middle of winter when I was selling drugs to this guy who seemed crazier than I was. I took his coat at gunpoint and left him in the middle of nowhere in West Seattle just to demonstrate how tough I thought I was. At the time, this seemed like gratitude for having a gun in my car when I was dealing with a crazy guy, and a foundational belief that you had to screw them before they screwed you because they definitely were a threat. In reality, it was just insecurity and a separation from my spiritual center that took me so far away from God that I did not know how I would ever get back. Today, I continue to just be grateful that I never had bullets in the gun.

Whether you are sliding down into the gutter or cesspool of life or upwardly spiraling to greatness, your dreams are based on just how thoroughly you know yourself through this inventory process. Step Five is about Allowing in your Dreams. I am not just talking about your lala-land-of-nod type dreams although those are fun to allow in. What I really am referring to are the dreams in waking hours, the big dreams like being an astronaut or in my case the President of the United States. What can I say? I was a precocious, gregarious child who just got bigger. My dreams of my childhood years got lost in the fog of boredom and apathy. I was looking for someone to simply make my dreams come true and didn't realize that responsibility was my own. In the absence of upward mobility and the insecurity of slowly coming to terms with being gay and whatever horrors that meant in my life, I was drawn into the underbelly of a dark life of drugs and sex. My dreams were nightmares. It was only after I went to prison and got clean off drugs that I was able to dream boldly again. I have no desire today to be an astronaut, but, who knows? I could still be President.

The dreams that recur over and over and in waking hours become what calls you and moves you forward. In Step Six, Crafting your Goals, you get to decide what it is you will do

Introduction

with your life. I frequently tell people I mentor, you can do anything you want in life as long as you are willing to pay the consequences. This "anything you want" is your set of goals. There was a time when I wanted to be a drug dealer and that is what I set out to do. My dreams were nightmares that bore the horror of my goals that put me behind bars. It isn't just the happy and wonderful things in life that are your goals. It is the dreams that get dreamt in waking hours over and over that become goals. It is important to be conscious about what you are putting your attention on and nurturing in the recesses of your mind. What has your waking attention? What you put your mind on grows like a garden getting water and fertilizer. The very root of intention is attention. Your goals are that attention.

The next step, Seven, is Setting the Plan. This can be as simple as making a list to get you to your goal. My list is usually something like go to Lowes, buy the wood needed for raised planter boxes, manhandle the wood home in a car unsuitable for the job, unload the wood to the back yard, stare at the pile for an uncomfortable amount of time, go inside, take a quick nap, forget about the goal in the first place, let the pile sit for a week or so until the struggle of looking at the pile reinvigorates the original goal, and Voila! Garden Boxes. Plans have been easy for me with goals that are straightforward like applying for a Doctoral program at Duke, starting a medical aesthetics practice, or building garden boxes. They are less easy to define when unwittingly the goal seems to be to attempt suicide because I am gay, to get addicted to drugs, or to go to prison. They may not have the elegant definition, yet they still exist. Even the spiral downward has intention built into it. This is the most important piece to remember about your life. Life is like a set of escalators, you are either going up, you are stuck on a floor, or you are going down. You can't just coast on an escalator.

The step before you get to celebrate your life is Step Eight, Taking Action. Without this step, your whole life is just a dream on paper stuck on some cloud somewhere, if you are lucky. Before I activated getting off drugs, I was drowning in the darkness of the sewer, just floating and sad. If you want to go somewhere, be someone, have something, you have to DO something. Life is a participation sport and it is your life, so you have to participate. How many times in my life have I felt like I was sidelined just observing life? How often did I feel like a victim without a voice? I slept for forty-two days straight in prison because I knew what action I could take and I didn't want to take any action at all. Amidst that inactivity, I put on weight, a lot of weight! Was I activating a plan there too? Was my goal to become obese? The activity and realization of negative goals are easiest to identify in retrospect. Reflecting on my life and knowing how and why I got there is only a consolation prize for letting my life be about horror and science fiction. To say that I did not know what I was doing because I was too far gone on drugs is a cop out and a lie. I knew what action to take and I chose to take different action because at the very root of the dreams was an inventory full of unworthiness, self-loathing, and lack.

Introduction

It would be very convenient to tell you that this process came to me very elegantly and neatly, that each of the nine steps was carefully laid out before me to craft into this book. The truth is that these steps were a product of a trial and lots of errors. I could only write this book from the perspective that I have today. My hope is that this book serves as a guide to anyone who may have or think they have a struggle with addiction, whether it be to drugs (including alcohol), sex, people, codependency, love, guilt, shame, trauma, shopping, adrenaline, writing, coffee, or work, just to name a few of mine. I may even have a few that I have not discovered yet. I know, however, that there is a process by which to live that brings me out of the dark prison cell of my past and into the shining light of hope for my future. This book is that process.

CHAPTER 1:

STRUGGLE

"If there is no struggle, there is no progress. Those who profess to favor freedom, and yet depreciate agitation, are men who want crops without plowing up the ground. They want rain without thunder and lightning. They want the ocean without the awful roar of its many waters. This struggle may be a moral one; or it may be a physical one; or it may be both moral and physical; but it must be a struggle. Power concedes nothing without a demand. It never did and it never will."
Frederick Douglass

The book slammed shut and I was cast into total darkness. Fear started to creep in as I realized my aloneness. I tried to move the oars of the boat. I needed to get away quickly, but there was no movement. My arms and legs would not move. My mind seemed separate from my body. Was I dead? Had my years of internal struggle finally culminated in my departure from this life? All of a sudden, I heard a sound and felt a presence. Again, fear coursed through my veins. I hoped the hideous pin-faced monster (Pinhead from the *Hellraiser* movie) that had been chasing me in the swamp had not caught up to me; I could not take any more of the fear and torment. In a futile effort, I tried to run. Nothing. I could not move. I was trapped in a weird and frightening series of near-death dreams.

Two narrow bands of light appeared before me

completely out of focus. It took a few heartbeats to realize that the lights were coming into once-lifeless eyes. Life and light blasting in from the loud room of my truly present moment.

A voice from above me grated my senses with a raspy-pitched croak, "We had a rough night last night," a frog-shaped face bellowed. I quickly took stock of my immobile body and realized I was restrained to the bed. My throat ached and I just wanted to reply, "No shit," but the words were drowned by my tears.

Back in my body, I returned to fear, embarrassment, and remorse quickly as I realized I was soaked in my own urine and lying in the bed completely exposed. The frog-faced nurse came into focus and intuitively sensed my fear. As my eyes focused, the frog turned into the angel who saved my life.

The raspy croak softened to a calm lilt. "Relax, you are safe. You are in the emergency room at Queen's Medical Center in Honolulu. You are going to be okay, now. We were not so sure last night. Do you remember anything? The medics brought you in without a heartbeat and we resuscitated you, a few times actually. You really were committed to checking out. You were found downtown on a sidewalk, unresponsive. Do you remember anything?"

"Not a thing, can I go now?" I pleaded through the fire in my throat. I was completely demoralized and humiliated having taken stock of my surroundings and condition. I was damp and stank and wanted to crawl away from the light of the room like a frightened cockroach. I was too

Chapter 1

young to die and too old to cry out for my mother, but in my fog that is what I really wanted—comfort.

Yes, I was in a fog, but lied about not remembering. I was too embarrassed to tell the nurse how a vacation in paradise turned into a vacation from hell. The things I remember were like flashes or snippets of a movie—a weird, frightening movie.

Twenty-Four Hours Earlier

I do remember being out with some people I met through Matthew, a flight attendant I met on my first day in Waikiki. I found these people fascinating and scary at the same time.

Matthew had to go back to work, leaving me alone with myself and my confusion. He left me with his friends, Athena and Scruff, who were instructed to care for me and show me a good time, whatever that might mean. Athena was sweet and caring in a convivial, Hawaiian way, but Scruff was attractive to me in a way that was indescribably dark and foreboding. It was Scruff who I wanted to show me a good time.

I was not sure whether Scruff was straight or gay. Heck, I was still trying to figure that out for myself. Scruff said he liked to "party" and I liked the way that sounded. I was on vacation and a party sounded great to me. I had no idea that tonight's party could have been my last.

Scruff and I went to a condo in downtown Waikiki to meet up with some people he "knew." These people dealt drugs, LSD to be exact and I liked LSD. I remember wanting to be liked and wanting to fit in. When Scruff asked me if I had ever done LSD before I just scoffed and said, "Of course." He warned me that this was concentrated and that I needed to be careful with it. What I didn't know is that Scruff was the supplier for these guys and he would fly this stuff in pure from another of the islands.

"Take the amount to fit on the head of a pin" was the instruction. "If some is good more must be better" was my mantra when it came to drugs. I put a dab of the powdered LSD on my finger. He warned me that was too much and made me brush some off, which I did, and then put my finger in my mouth like a pacifier set to take away my feelings. My feelings were more frightening than the drugs. My feelings were about being different. My feelings were about Matthew and my sexuality. I just wanted to dream of my life being different so I did the drugs. It could have been my last time; I overdosed.

The last conscious memory I have of that evening was looking down at my hand in shock. I had ripped out a big hunk of my own hair and was screaming, "I am losing my mind." I was. Flashes of light were coming at me all too fast. I was so overwhelmed with my life and the chemicals that coursed unabated through my brain, my young brain. I think I remember feeling like I was going into the unknown and then it all went dark. I did dream, frightening horrible dreams. I was dreaming that death was coming.

Clearly, the dealers were uncomfortable having a twenty-something young man overdosing in their condo. They were drug dealers after all and had a certain image to uphold.

I guess they took me downstairs and were good enough to call 911 while I lay on the cold, hard sidewalk struggling for my life. The pages in the book of my life flipped backwards slowly …

Why I Went to Waikiki

How I got to that point in the late spring of 1986 was through a series of life steps that are somewhat difficult to tease apart and retell. What I remember is that apart from anything else, I truly wanted to be normal and by normal, I really mean that in the mid-1980s I wanted to be heterosexual. So for all outward appearances, I dated women hoping that they would not uncover my true struggles.

Sometimes struggles are so hard to unravel because it is difficult to determine where they started. As I worked on writing this book, I realized that struggle is an offshoot or a next step in the cycle after Celebration, which I discuss at length in a future chapter.

So going back to the Celebration before this struggle would be turning back the story to where I asked Sara, a wonderful girl I met in college, if she would consider someday saying yes if I proposed. It wasn't a "true" proposal because I was still internally struggling with my sexuality. I gave Sara a small but flawless diamond ring that I'd bought with money I had made in Amsterdam as a prostitute in 1985 when I was there alone on a month-long "vacation."

I worked in the Blue Boy Club just off Dam Square in Amsterdam. I was cute and very young and could usually convince any of the desperate Johns there to buy me a drink and some hash and then take them to a back room to give them a private show and let them take care of themselves. For that, I was handsomely paid, at least enough to buy a diamond and live quite well for a few weeks in the city.

I guess I thought the diamond would somehow purify my thoughts and past transgressions, maybe even my future transgressions. I knew that there was something unchangeable within me that made such a promise impossible to keep; however, I believed perhaps it was a struggle I might win if I was enough of a warrior.

My warrior pose, though, was that of a scared, lost boy trying to fit into unfittable situations. I was a fraud and I knew it.

Back in the United States, I lived in a prestigious fraternity on campus and was almost asked to leave because I drank too much. In the late 1980s, it was assumed one would drink in a fraternity but I was taking it to the extreme.

Often after an evening of drinking or smoking pot, I would find myself on a bus to Capitol Hill—the gay part of town. All at once, my cloak of discomfort would slip away and I would feel oddly at home in a world I still considered dark and taboo.

I was living a double life stuck between two mountains and struggling to avoid becoming lost in the valley in-between. I cared for Sara, but at the same time I was compelled to explore this other side of myself. I had been

Chapter 1

living this double life for two years and it was taking its toll on me and on Sara.

Sara noticed my moodiness as I inwardly struggled. I felt the devastation of possibly losing this sweet angel from my life mixed with the horrible deliciousness of possibly being gay. I decided I needed some time alone away from Seattle to think things through.

So, I went to Waikiki by myself.

My mind was made up. I was gay, case and closet closed!

When I look back on this time in my life, I recognize that many of my struggles are rooted in some way in my struggle with my sexuality. Drugs and alcohol were the "tools" I used to fit into situations where I felt uncomfortable being "straight." Drugs made me more self-accepting of being "gay."

Struggle in My Early Years

As my life's journey moved from my innocent youth toward that fateful night on the sidewalk in Waikiki, I increasingly found myself catapulted into dark and desperate corners. They were the kind of corners where many people become trapped and do not get out from alive. My story is most likely different from yours yet there are identifiable patterns for many people I have shared these things with. We all have a story of struggle, surrender, and coming of age. It is the story of the Prodigal Son or the Hero's Journey.

I thought I was a normal teenager. I had no one in my life to compare myself to. My parents had left almost a full generation gap between my sisters and me, or so it felt. By the time I came along, they were out of practice for knowing what was normal for a teenager and really had no preparation for dealing with the teenage boy species. Time-lapse between siblings can truly wash away all "sins" that children are commonly known for. I am not talking about sin in the Old Testament sort of way, although some could ultimately argue that, in my case, I am. I am speaking about the sins of a teenager. I never thought of it as anything but good teenage fun.

I had awareness in my early teens of right and wrong. Right and wrong may be overstating it a bit. I had awareness of "in trouble" or "not in trouble." Sometimes it was more like "in trouble" or "getting praised." I was never described as a bad child. Quite the contrary, most people, adults that is, had the perception that George Lytton Baxter III was a good kid—wholesome, polite, mature, and funny. I was a Boy Scout, an Eagle Scout, a football player, Honor Roll. I had convinced everyone I was a perfect child, yet there was a sense of mischievousness behind the green shorts, neckerchief, and merit badges. I had struggled with this double life early on, not knowing that it would ultimately be my undoing.

I wish I could say that this Jekyll and Hyde personality started in my teens, but as I look back, I realize it began much earlier. You know when you almost catch a child red-handed at something naughty and you ask, "What are you doing?" Then they try to disarm you with the sweetest, singsong reply of "nothing" and bat their innocent eyes at

Chapter 1

you in a sort of hypnotic way until you forget the original act. That was me. Trouble did not find me like some external devil, but was nurtured from within me as a way to push boundaries and test limits.

I remember a spring night when I was seven or maybe eight. Let's just say I was old enough to know better. I pray this will not be my epitaph. My friends and I were out playing flashlight tag and it was almost dark enough to really get the game going. I have no idea what came over me, but I suddenly found myself standing in the kitchen of our house on Long Island with a lighter in my hand lighting the paper towels on fire above the dishwasher. I ran out the door.

Where did I get the lighter? What was the purpose of trying to burn the house down? Funny thing, although I have thought about that story a lot of times, I don't think I have made an admission about it until now. What is the Statute of Limitations on being an arsonist? I wonder.

I just thought I was a normal kid, a well-behaved, fun-loving, normal kid from a good home with a good family, a regular "Leave it to Beaver" upbringing. I guess even Jerry Mathers had a dark-side though, right?

The lighter was my mother's. She smoked from as early as I can recall. It was cool until it wasn't. I took drastic measures to convince her to quit smoking, including explosions. Back in the day (a phrase that always makes me feel old) they had spikes you could put into the tip of a cigarette to make it explode when it was ignited. They were meant as pranks, but probably not the best way for an eight-year-old to convince his mom that smoking was no longer cool. After the first one exploded, I decided that the most appropriate action would be to confess that there was a second charge planted deeper in the pack. Not to get anyone in trouble, but I think that corporal punishment was how that story ended.

The pendulum on smoking swung the other way for both my mother and me. When I was fifteen, she finally decided to quit smoking. She threw away the last four cigarettes in her Vantage Ultra Light Menthol pack. I dug those cigarettes out of the trash. Those were the first four cigarettes I smoked as a committed smoker. Thank you, Mom.

Is it just me or is the head-spinning projectile vomiting worse from menthol than it is from regular cigarettes? With every drag of those leftovers, I felt cooler and freer. In my head, I was writing new commercial copy for happiness. I wasn't struggling anymore but had surrendered to this wonderful feeling of freedom. The bonus feature was the profound dizziness. My solution was to switch to Marlboro Lights.

It is not easy to be good on the outside, bad on the inside and smell like cigarette smoke. I had already surrendered to keeping up my image as a good kid. Now I also had surrendered to the feeling of being terminally cool from smoking. This dichotomy led to finding creative ways to cover the smell and keep my image. Turns out, I had four basic tools: Polo cologne, hand soap, fresh air, and grape Bubble Yum. To this day, I link the smell of artificial grape to Marlboro Lights.

It is funny how there are certain smells that will always

Chapter 1

stick with you for life, literally like bad memories—like mothballs at my Grandmother Mimi's house or the smell of urine while walking to the bus stop. Although urine is a prevalent smell in Manhattan, it is not so common on Long Island; at least it wasn't in the early seventies, except for me and one friend.

I am not as mortified to admit it as I have been, but I wet the bed until I was almost twelve, and a few unrelated times in college. The unrelated college times were because I drank too much, a lack of social not physical control. I have come to find out that many kids wet the bed past the point where they "should," but how was I supposed to know that then. It is not like there was some formal club set up for adolescent bed-wetters so that we could all gather in the stench of urine and feel for the first time like we belonged.

I remember as a very small child a sort of Chinese fire drill that happened each morning. My bed would be stripped down to the telltale plastic mattress cover and tossed in the wash with my pajama onesie while I stood there naked, exposed, alone, and helpless. Feeling degradation and insecurity for the first time and having no language to express it except tears. Unfortunately, I got better at experiencing degradation and insecurity over the years.

Then one day walking to the bus stop, it hit me like the sweet fragrance of community. I came out of the house in time to meet up with my friend Nathan from up the street. As we walked the quarter mile to the corner of Van Brunt Manor Road and Shore Road, a familiar smell whispered in my nostrils. "Do you wet your bed, too?" I asked. With an affirmative nod, we both felt a glimmer of acceptance, maybe for the first time. A friendship was born.

Nathan was a "bad" kid, according to my mother. She would make proclamations about people like this that would only make me find them more interesting. Mr. Hyde had his curiosity piqued, "Bad?" Because I struggled with wanting to be "bad" and "good" at the same time, I needed someone in my life who would take the focus off my "bad."

The story Mom continues to tell that exemplifies her feelings about Nathan happened when we were in Webelos, the step before Boy Scouts. My father was one of our Webelos leaders and there was a trip planned to New York City to tour Radio City Music Hall, the World Trade Center, and the Empire State Building. We took the train into the city, which for Nathan and me had the familiar smell of urine mixed with something yet to be defined.

My detective friend Nathan found the source, an almost-finished pint of rum. There was just enough left in the bottom so we could all smell like New York City by the time we arrived at the Manhattan station. Nathan mischievously sprinkled our uniforms with rum. A bold move on Nathan's part, my hero. Dr. Jekyll would never let me be so bold. Image was too important even at eleven years old.

Those foundational years in Webelos taught me many great lessons. Not the least of which was to always have friends who were considered "bad" kids. Not only was it more conducive to being able to have more fun, but also provided reasonable and plausible scapegoats should the need arise and the need did frequently arise.

Chapter 1

I wonder if the Boy Scouts of America ever considered adding the merit badges of smoking, drinking, and public disorderly conduct to the ever-growing list of merit badge possibilities. I would have received my Eagle Scout much sooner if they had, rather than waiting until hours before the deadline of my eighteenth birthday.

No matter how you think a Boy Scout should behave, the truth is every troop member is just itching to get into trouble of one sort or another and limit supervision. In fact, my first brush with the law was in Boy Scouts.

I can't remember if we stole the liquor from the VFW (where our troop met) to get drunk while selling Christmas trees or if those were two separate incidents: the liquor stealing and the getting drunk. I do know that the booze heist was not me. I left that up to the "bad" kids.

All I remember is that I could not wait until 9:00 p.m. when our Christmas tree stand would be closed down for sales for the evening. We had to spend the night on the lot to make sure the trees were safe. I'm very sure that they were. It's amazing how quickly you can get drunk at that age. Stupidity is compounded exponentially by immaturity and the undrinkable ratio of rum to coke; going for a walk around town seemed like a good idea.

It doesn't really matter what goofy mischief we got into around the small town of Vashon that night. Quite frankly, I am sure none of us remember. The only clear memory I have is standing behind the Vashon Island Theatre. We were staring at this cool mural of some film strips painted with old movie star faces. As we stood there giggling and swaying in the alley behind the theater, Greta Garbo's face seemed to light up as if she were on stage. The downstage light was coming from the car of the King County Sheriff inquiring about just exactly what we were up to that night. Busted! And so, it began…

Struggle is Good

Everyone struggles to one degree or another. Some even define themselves by their struggles. "I am a cancer survivor" or "I am a starving student." Perhaps at times we all define ourselves by our struggles.

I have hesitated to include this as a step in the process, partially due to the propensity for morbidity around being stuck in the struggle and partly because I just don't want to have to admit that there have been struggles in my life. That was before I found the positive side of struggle. The fact is that when all is said and done, it is about not being stuck but using struggle as a tool, a step, an essential element of living with intention.

I refer to struggle as a first step; however, this connotes more of an upward and linear process than I am intending. The process is much more obtuse than linear, and struggle is merely a point on a circular continuum. After all, every story needs a start and struggle is as good a place to start as any. When someone asks, "You want the good news first or the bad news?" I believe that most people want to get the bad news out of the way so they can celebrate the good news.

Chapter 1

I don't believe struggle can be judged as bad or good, although that was not always the case. I can remember many times feeling like a victim of circumstance and struggling with struggle. When you are wrestling a big overwhelming reptile, it is almost impossible to focus on anything else. When you are in the middle of struggle, it has you hostage, hopeless, and helpless. The goal of struggle is to not stay in the middle of it. You need to wiggle at your bonds and move to the outer edges where you can finally be free. However, struggle is necessary for changing a life. It is through struggle that the whole downward spiral can collapse on itself to spring forth anew. If struggle cannot be judged as bad or good and is necessary for positive change then from a spiritual perspective one would have to say that struggle is inherently Good without opposite. Next time you are in the middle of it, remind yourself of that. Say to yourself, "This is God, this is Good, this has no opposite, thank you." I recommend trying it out on the small stuff first like missing a traffic light or oversleeping your alarm.

Struggle is that resistance and friction that is known through the way it feels. It is difficult to fully sense struggle with the traditional ways of sensing. It is more subtle than seeing or hearing struggle, although your senses will obviously take in input that can help your inner sense know that you are there in the midst of struggle.

Struggle can be generally categorized into four distinct life areas: health, wealth, relationships, and creative expression. Maybe as you read this book you will come up with an area of struggle that falls outside these four areas, but I have yet to find one, perhaps because of my very broad definitions of these areas.

Health is an all-encompassing realm of wellbeing. It is physical and mental wellness. Much of what we do and are exposed to can affect this area of life. The food we eat, how we eat it, our environment, where we live, who we surround ourselves with can all negatively or positively affect our health. Some of the biggest struggles and changes I have made in my life fall into this area. As the name of this book suggests—*Drugs, Food, Sex and God*—three out of four of these topics have had a dramatically negative effect on my health and wellbeing.

Wealth relates mostly to money or what money represents. Struggles around money are so pervasive for people that it really doesn't matter how much money you might have—you can find yourself smack dab in the middle of struggle around wealth issues. Uncovering some of the baggage that we have around the topic of wealth is important to live in a new paradigm that allows us to let go of the struggle around money. As I wrote this book, I realized that my struggles with drugs, sex, and money were wrapped up in my old messages about self-worth. I strived to get more and more in a way that ultimately led me to prison.

Relationships are the spice of life. The relationship struggles many of us have are with those who are closest to us. However, I believe that we all have a primary relationship with ourselves, and all other relationships are reflections back to that one. As I take a look back on the relationships I have had in my life, both intimate and non-intimate, I find that each of them is peppered with the quality of self-worth I had at the time.

Finally, creative expression is an expansive area of life where you find your connection with God. What brings you passion? What is your calling? How have you been led to do the work that you are doing in the world? Each of these questions is important for feeling empowered through self-expression and creative expression. I am not talking about your job, unless your job is your passion and your calling. Most people don't refer to their passion as just a job.

Not every struggle has to be a life or death challenge to be a pivotal moment in your life. Struggle shows up in many different ways. Struggle sometimes feels overwhelming with no end in sight. There is only one way out of struggle and on we go to Surrender.

CHAPTER 2:

Surrender

"Each time we let go, there is a degree of mourning and then an opening of possibility."
Narcotics Anonymous, *Living Clean: The Journey Continues*

Surrender can take on an infinite number of shapes and forms—some good, some bad, and every adjective in between. Some view surrender as a complete failure. Others consider it a letting go. The most elegant definition I have found for surrender is "coming over to the winning side." Surrender is something we do every day. Actually, we do it to start our day. We surrender to being awake; we set aside our desire to sleep and dream, to face the new day ahead. If you view surrender as a "bad" thing then waking up may be one of the hardest things you do all day. If, on the other hand, you see yourself getting out of bed on the winning side then the day is yours to make with it what you will.

This book is not about the little surrenders although it certainly could be. This book is about life-changing, course-altering surrenders that come from not living in integrity with the very essence of life itself. I was caught in a life of lies and my whole existence was in a state of resistance. My health and wellbeing suffered at physical, spiritual, mental, and emotional levels.

The first thing that I surrendered to was escape. I used

drugs and alcohol to change how I felt about my world and myself, hoping that surrendering would make my world easier to live in. Alcohol, and later drugs, made me feel I was on the winning side. I was able to live my life in an artificially induced carefree state. I did not realize the damage I was doing to the very core of my connectedness with the Universe.

Escape would continue to be my fallback position whenever life was too hard, too fast, too complicated, or too … Tuesday. I guess I never really needed an excuse to try and escape; I had been trying to escape my entire life. I didn't understand the feelings I had as a young boy growing up. I didn't know why I felt so different and so wrong. I knew that something had to give but I had no idea what it was. Finding out about what it was to be gay became easier through a rampant use of drugs and alcohol. If I were to select anything to change about my life, it would be this particular fact. I have surrendered to the ultimate fact that looking back on the entirety of my life so far, it has been a purposeful life on a clear path, lined up like a key in lock tumblers.

Matthew was my first real boyfriend although I had "experiences" prior to Matthew. Sara was not my last girlfriend. Seem confusing? Try living it! I thought that when I met Matthew I would finally come out of the closet and never go back. I thought that I had that ultimate surrender to my sexuality there on the beach in Waikiki. I was wrong.

I was twenty-two when I gave up alcohol for the first time and surrendered to my first Twelve Step recovery experience. I loved the feeling of thinking and living clean. My mind was clearing and I was motivated for the future. I had a good job as an assistant manager at a clothing store and I was saving money for the first time. It seemed that everything in my life was going well. I was discovering things about myself through the process of the Twelve Steps. I guess deep down I thought that there might be a step out of the twelve that would change me into something different, sexually, something that at the very core I was not. I had a very difficult time with acceptance.

I was on a trip with my sponsor and 349 other sober people at Club Med. What an experience for a newly sober young, energetic man. It is truly amazing how truly insane sober people can be. If I didn't know better I would have thought they were drunk, but I was able to truly experience fun without alcohol on a beach, in the sun, in Mexico. I met some wonderful people that week but the one I remember the most was a woman named Jennifer.

Jennifer and I shared our stories with each other late into the evening. We hung out together. We were inseparable. We were even partners in the Guest Talent Show dancing the Lambada, a very hot and sexual Brazilian dance. Did she know she was hanging out with a gay man? I mean, I was not a loafer-wearing, lisping, swishy, fashion-conscious, flag-waving, committed gay man, but I had made my "choice." Did she know? Something happened in my brain that week and I thought that Jennifer was my way out, my redemption, my "unchoosing." I didn't realize that she would be my ultimate surrender to who I really was.

I told her everything about my history. Everything. She knew about Matthew and about all of my exploits. I was completely honest with her but she was still hellbent on dating a gay man, a semi-committed gay man. I was wavering. It didn't feel like it was an "I think I can change him" relationship but maybe it was. All I knew was that I was up for her challenge. After all, it would change the one thing about my being that was the most difficult for me to accept and surrender to, the one thing that drove all others. If I could just magically change into a straight man then I would live happily ever after. Jennifer and I would live in the suburbs with 2.5 children and a Volvo station wagon. I would be on the town council and she would be president of the PTA. The sun would come out every day and create happy rainbows that would kerfuffle out of my ass everywhere I went. Oh, what a life that would be. Wrong!

We carried on a longish-distance relationship between Los Angeles and San Francisco and would split our time visiting each other in both locations. I don't think that I cheated on Jennifer with any of the men in my life and I would like to think that I was really giving this new lie a real try. I remember one weekend we had planned to go up to Seattle for a big convention together. We were going to stay at my parents' house and Jennifer was going to meet George and Carol for the first time. I am quite certain that my parents didn't quite know what to think about me bringing home a girlfriend although I am sure they were elated.

Chapter 2

I don't know what came over me that weekend or if it was something that I heard at the convention. Perhaps I heard a speaker getting truly honest about who they were and how they loved themselves for all of it. It was as if a switch was finally turned on for me. Jennifer and I drove back to my parents' house in relative silence. I may have been brooding; I do that sometimes when I have something weighty on my mind. We pulled into the driveway and parked the car. I felt the pressure building inside me and I knew I was going to burst. I also knew that I really did not want to have the next conversation in the house with my parents listening. As we got out of the car and started up the walk, I held Jennifer's hand. I turned her so we were face to face and I stared into her eyes. I needed her to know that I was certain and that I did not waver.

"Jennifer, I can't do this anymore. I feel like I am lying to myself and to you. Continuing on like this is only going to hurt both of us."

"I know," was her only response.

That was the just the beginning of the final surrender for me to my sexuality. I knew that I would find a way to love myself for all of it. I had no idea how long it would take or the depths to which I would plummet before that happened.

My friend Ester Nicholson writes in her book, *Soul Recovery: 12 Keys to Healing Addiction*, "Real surrender itself is not painful. Genuine surrender is blissful. It is our resistance to giving up control that's difficult." For many years to come I was still firmly planted in the resistance and wanting the bliss.

Not knowing how I would get to a place where I could or would love myself, I guess I threw myself into my "work." After that time of brief sobriety, I found that acceptance of oneself was easier when I was high. I surrendered to that fact and started using drugs with reckless abandon. There is a disconnect, however, with rampant drug use and not having a consistent job although rampant drug use does make employability dicey to say the least. I did find some "freelance" work in sales and marketing, at least that is what I called it for resume building.

Selling little packages to my friends allowed all of us to get high, but a greater opportunity lurked in the shadows. It's like the guy who goes to the corner store to buy a case of beer for his friends and realizes for the first time that it's the storeowner who is really prospering from them having a good time. Maybe that is a lousy analogy because I have no clue what the mark-up on beer is. The mark-up on methamphetamines is extraordinary.

Methamphetamines can be manufactured just about anywhere using common household poisons and, in some cases, cold medicine. The total cost of production is about $200 per pound of meth. By the time the finished product reached me from Mexico, the price would have risen to a street value of around $15,000 per pound.

I really have no clue how it would go from the manufacturing stage in Mexico to me across the border and honestly did not care at that time. Some of the stories were spine-tingling. These stories came to me second or third-hand so I can't account for the accuracy. The truth about the stories is that I did hear them.

Chapter 2

All of the stories had a common theme, the Mexican Mafia. I just have to assume that this was a real entity, although no one ever showed up at my door and presented a calling card. That would have been hysterical, but probably not at the time. At that time in my "career," I had a healthy fear of death, dismemberment, the cops, and anything else related to the elusive Mexican Mafia.

All I know is that I was warned that I would be taken care of if I didn't follow directions and well taken care of if I did. So I did. My contact was a guy in Seattle named John (that was not his real name). He and I forged a friendship, such as it was. I wanted so much to think it was a friendship, but in retrospect, I believe that would be horribly overstating things.

It was pre-9/11 and life was very different. John instructed me to get a hotel room in an upscale hotel in Seattle under an assumed name and pay cash, something that would be unthinkable today. I would call him and give him my name, address, room number, and then I would hang out and wait for a shipment via FedEx. I remember partying in a fancy hotel in downtown Seattle for three days in a Junior Suite waiting anxiously for my package.

When the package arrived, John would come by the hotel. He was always neatly dressed with slacks and a nice collared shirt. He looked professional and carried a briefcase. He certainly didn't look like your typical drug-dealing mafia guy, whatever that was supposed to look like. I remember liking his style and the way he carried himself. I never saw him do the drugs he bought and looking back on it, that was probably the secret of his "success." Perhaps I would still be in that world if I chose the same route as John, another reason to be eternally grateful for my particular path in life.

When John came by, then and only then, I could open the package and sample the goods. It actually was required of me to test it out and make sure that it was good. I remember feeling so much bigger than life at the time, like a made-for-TV movie. There were pounds of methamphetamines in my hotel room. I would leave with my pound and start my rounds. I would always have my people ready and waiting for me to meet up with them. This life was the perfect replacement life for the life I had wanted and I found myself falling into the bliss of surrendering to it. But the bliss was artificially and intravenously induced and could not last.

Somewhere in the dark hours of my life, I remember asking for help. I didn't know to what or to whom I was asking this question and didn't really believe help would come. I just remember that I knew that I would not stay alive if I kept living that way. Each action I took seemed more dangerous than the last. I didn't care about the people I was with. I didn't care that I had started carrying a gun with me everywhere. I didn't even know why.

"Please help me."

This simple prayer is all that is needed to voice surrender. The wheels that were set in motion by this prayer are indescribable. The Universe, which is always conspiring for my benefit, had my back and it knew what needed to be done to pluck me from these depths. I was arrested, judged, found guilty, appealed, and my appeal was denied. Physical surrender was all that was left for me.

A chapter on surrender in a book about an ex-felon would not be complete without the story of "giving myself up." I was released on my own recognizance after being found guilty, pending the outcome of my appeal. The appeal didn't go my way. Let's just say that being arrested and found guilty of dealing drugs is not at all like they portray it in the movies, at least it wasn't for me.

It was a day like any other day, really. I was using drugs and hiding their use from my boyfriend at the time. He must have just thought that I had a lot of energy all the time. Anyway, this was the day that I had decided I would turn myself in at the county jail to start serving my prison sentence. The process goes like this; you are booked and processed at the county jail, transported to the state facility where you are processed some more, and then you wait to be transferred again to another place where the processing continues.

There is a biblical nature to the last day of freedom. Meth addicts aren't much for "last suppers" because they don't eat. (This is why they all look so super-model skinny.) There is a procession though. I had my boyfriend drive me around to various "friends" so I could say my goodbyes. At each stop, there was an offering of drugs in a symbolic gesture of farewell. I don't think that the rules are actually written anywhere, but this story is not unique. Funny thing is that the same procession happens when a felon gets out of prison too. Because my boyfriend did not know that I used drugs intravenously, I would excuse myself to the bathroom at each house to use in private.

It was starting to get late and I had one final stop to make—my best friend's house. He was also a very good customer of mine and one of the people I would miss the most while I was away. We would say that I was going away to camp, which made it sound so much better. I realized when we got to his house that with all of the procession and bathroom stops, I had neglected to eat and was starting to get lightheaded.

I asked my friend for a going-away gift (more drugs), the use of his bathroom, and something to eat. He was able to oblige me with the "gift" and the bathroom, but only had shredded carrot salad to eat. You certainly do not go over to a meth house and expect to find gourmet food or food at all for that matter. It was good carrot salad though. I ate it like it was a last supper.

Finally, it was time to go. It was time to turn myself in, give myself up. I was in full-on drama mode. It is just in my gay genes. We all said our goodbyes. There were some tears shed and then in the vacuum that was my departure, new tweakers would take my place and I was soon forgotten.

My boyfriend dropped me downtown and we said our private goodbyes. We hugged for a long time and cried together. This man actually was a rock for me through all of this and it is something that I will always be grateful for. He was going to take care of my cats, Anna and Abigale, for me while I was away at "camp" and he would be my link to the outside world.

Chapter 2

It was time … what time was it? Oh, my God, it was 1:30 in the morning. The procession of goodbyes was really long and time just slipped away. Lucky for me jail is a twenty-four hour business. I had no idea exactly how this worked so I just walked up to the back door of the jail in downtown Seattle and knocked. I knocked again. And again. A guard finally came to the door. Apparently, the graveyard shift guard wasn't used to people knocking on the back door to the jail. It's not really a place people are pounding the door down to get into. And there I was, pounding on the door.

"Um, can I do something for you?" the guard stammered at me with a surprised voice. He had either just woken up or truly thought I was some wild-eyed crazy dude trying to break into jail.

"I am here to turn myself in," I stated with more confidence than I was feeling at the time. I was surrendering and I felt nauseous about it.

He let me through the first door into an empty no man's land. There is always a reason for rooms like this. It can't just be poor design. It looked like a foyer of sorts with a locked door at both sides. The only thing in the room with me was a cardboard box top that looked like it used to hold a case of pop.

"Wait here," he said with a disapproving look and he disappeared behind door number two. Clearly, I had disturbed his usual routine.

As I stood there waiting, I started to feel more and more nauseous. I thought it was just nerves but there came that point of realization that this was bigger than just nervousness. Clearly being nervous would have made sense; I was turning myself in for the first time after all. New experiences always gave me a sense of excited trepidation.

Nervousness morphed from nauseous to the flavor of carrot as I realized I might actually be sick soon. One of the reasons that I was so happy to quit was because I hated throwing up. The funny thing about it though is that it doesn't really matter how you feel about this particular bodily function. If it is going to happen, there is nothing you can do about it.

I saw the guard eyeing me from behind the glass as my brain was reeling with what my next logical steps might be. I wonder what picture he saw as he watched some saucer-eyed crazy man fighting to control his gag reflex. In my mind, the picture was cool. Poised even. When I was high, I had this image that I looked a lot like James Bond doing just about anything. Throwing up in jail would be no different. Then it happened.

My friend's dry carrot salad made a rather quick transition from resting uncomfortably in my churning stomach to completely filling my mouth. My cheeks puffed out like a chipmunk's but James Bond did not throw up. It was a slow motion controlled smooth suave dance that took me over to the box top to let the carrots free. With a thud, this hideously large ball of dry carrots fell out of my mouth and hit the cardboard. Double O Seven didn't even have to wipe his mouth; it was that cool.

The overhead speaker crackled and the guard said

Chapter 2

disgustedly, "You are going to have to leave and come back during the day." The door behind me buzzed and my freedom lay outside. All that procession was wasted and so was I. Surrender did not go so well that time.

I had to think about what to do next. I could call my boyfriend to come get me and do this whole day over. Just the thought of having to say goodbye again made me to feel weak; I had really given the last goodbye my all. I decided to call my friend with the carrot salad to come get me. I was hungry again after all. Also, at his house I could use drugs the way I wanted without hiding it.

I was never given a specific day when I had to turn myself in so I spent the next three days repainting the outside of my friend's garage until he let me know that it was time to give myself up again. It almost felt like he was trying to get rid of me. No one gets rid of James Bond, especially when he is painting your garage. Just after noon, he dropped me off in front of the county jail at a more appropriate time without any drama or fanfare.

Real surrender does not have to be painful or dramatic.

When I can let go of the notion that I might know what is right for my life then amazing things can happen. Today, I know that those amazing things are God, Universal Spirit, Energy. Whatever you want to call it. I know that all it takes is getting out of the way and letting go of being so cool, James. Just let go. That is what surrender is. It is in the letting go that the path is made clear.

Years later, after some time clean, I chose to surrender to something positive. I decided to get my Masters in Nursing from the University of Washington. I thought I wanted to be a nurse practitioner so I applied to that program. As a second choice, I also applied to the Clinical Nurse Specialist track in the nursing school because either way I was furthering my nursing career. I didn't get accepted to the nurse practitioner program so I let go of that idea and dove into the CNS program.

I found out that after the first year in the CNS program it was possible to transfer to the nurse practitioner program if you were the right candidate. I didn't know then what I truly wanted to do, but what I did know was that the Universe had my back and all I needed to do was the work, in this case, a lot of schoolwork.

I surrendered to the work and excelled in my classes. I loved the work and the material and because of that love, I did well. I also did well because there was a group of us who studied together and helped each other get through those first classes. Physical Biology 1 and 2 were rough, but our little band stuck together and all of us excelled. I came up with crazy ways of remembering skin disorders and kidney issues, but we all remembered the crazy so it worked.

I reached a point in the program where I was eligible to put in a transfer to the Nurse Practitioner Program. I didn't know at that time, but the transfer had already been processed. Two of my professors recognized that I would make a great nurse practitioner and had put in the transfer on my behalf. All I did was the work. I surrendered.

Surrender does not have to be dramatic. It is an opening

Chapter 2

and an allowing to the possibilities of life. Once we let go of the struggle and drop the masks and defenses, then life can take over. Surrender leaves a void where struggle used to exist. We are naturally driven to fill the void. There has to be a sense of purpose that can only come from believing we are worthy of having the void filled in the most miraculous ways. The next step in our journey is Belief.

CHAPTER 3:

Belief

"Follow your bliss and the universe will open doors for you where there were only walls."
Joseph Campbell.

It doesn't matter in what you believe; everyone has a belief in something. When we hear the word "belief" many of us think of God or some dogmatic icon where we can prayerfully place our order or submit our wish list. We wait to see if our prayers are answered like some cosmic restaurant. I hope not to offend anyone when I unabashedly state that God is not Santa Claus. There is no naughty and nice list and there is no boogieman waiting to rob you of your soul.

Belief is more ubiquitous than just a reliance on God, Spirit, or some universal principle. We believe in an almost continuous fashion in others and nature and sometimes even ourselves.

As I write this, I am on an airplane going to visit my mother-in-law in Texas. I believe in the pilot to take off, fly, and land safely. I believe that when I ask for coffee from "Kim," my flight attendant, that I will get coffee and that her name really is Kim, although the only proof I have is her nametag. Belief takes on a life of its own and doesn't need to have proof to be so. This is the difference between belief and hope or trust.

There is something essentially calming about belief for

me. When I have hope that something will happen or trust that something will not happen there is just an inkling of insecurity, doubt, or angst. Sometimes what I hope for doesn't happen or what I trust won't happen does—darn, darn, darn. But belief is like a cool lake on a warm day: refreshing and consistent. There is no turbulence and no monsters, just the cooling waters of absolute divine patterning. This holds true no matter what you believe in.

Growing up I had no idea what to believe. I went to church as a tagalong with my mother who served as the church organist at many of the churches in the Stony Brook area. Presbyterian, Episcopalian, Jewish Temple, and Methodist were all different flavors of the same story as far as I was concerned. I went to Sunday school to give my mother a chance to play without me singing along with songs I didn't really know (or like). I think I still sing along to songs I don't know. In Sunday school, I learned about Jesus or at least what he looked like and I must have been on the lookout for him like some religious fanatic. "He will come again in glory...," they just never said when.

In the early 1970s, the boys were all trying to grow their facial hair as some sort of rebellion. At four, I was not one of those boys. I never understood the whole facial hair thing. Perhaps it was because I once asked my father to teach me how to shave and he told me that he would when I needed to know. To this day, I don't know if I know how to shave correctly and don't care. Every man in his early twenties had as long a beard as they could grow. I remember walking through the "emergency ice cream"

Chapter 3

grocery store with my mother after church one Sunday. As we shopped, I stopped a young man in the middle of the aisle and loudly squealed, "Are you Jesus?" I believed he was coming and I believed it was now.

I was four then and things slowly changed. I went from seeing Jesus in the grocery store to thinking I was Jesus while high on LSD somewhere in my twenties. Eventually, I was just praying to a God I didn't really believe in to get me out of the mess that I had made of my life.

I remember standing in the courtroom in front of Justice Bridge. My attorney had already laid out a case whereby the court could really "throw the book" at me. I don't really remember all of the ins and outs of what he was telling me just that there did not seem to be any option other than serving time in prison.

It was in this wood-paneled room where I realized that I could believe in the system. I can't explain what came over me, but somehow I knew that no matter what happened and what the final verdict was, I would be okay.

When the guilty verdict was reached, there was no surprise. I was calm really. I knew that I would be found guilty. The police had set up listening devices on the phone at one of my customers' houses and had "convinced" Michael, the customer, to cooperate with their plan to reel in a "big fish." I guess I should be flattered that they considered me so important.

Funny side note about the big fish, it was a slippery one. It just so happens that the day when Michael called for me to bring some "stuff" was my birthday, March 2, 1996 and being a reasonable businessman, I was taking my birthday off. I sent one of my people to go in my place and the police did end up with a "fish," just not me! They didn't get me this time, but …

It wasn't long before another customer was "persuaded" to cooperate with the police. It was only a matter of time before I was going to be caught for doing what I was doing. Drug dealers who don't think they will get caught and don't think that what they are doing is really hurting anyone, spend too much time in "don't think." Belief is crafted by what we do think, not by what we don't think.

It was my sense of belief that kept me from getting caught for so long, not a belief that I was unstoppable or invincible. Injecting meth every day does make you feel like you have superhuman strength. Superhuman until your bones and muscles start to cannibalize themselves and your teeth fall out of your head, not to mention the skin picking … all very glamorous. I actually believed in myself and my way of doing business as crazy as this sounds. Remember, for every act of intention to the positive there is an equal and opposite act of intention to the negative. Intention is without judgment, like a principle or a force in nature.

I had ways of dealing that were tried, true, and slippery to catch. In fact, they were only able to charge me with "possession with intent" because they never did catch me in the act. This book might be very different had that not been the case. I certainly would not have had the opportunity to turn my life around and would have been in prison for a much longer time.

Along with this belief that I was a good drug dealer was

Chapter 3

a belief that I would be able to stop using and dealing at any given moment. I just didn't want to yet. The biggest lie addicts tell themselves is "I can stop when I want." Wrong! I was trying to get enough money together to buy a house and settle down. I guess I believed that if I had those things life would somehow be better. Frequently, I found myself having to put my belief in things and people outside myself.

Now I believed that Judge Bobbe Bridge was going to care for me. I hoped that I would not get prison time, but there is the difference again between hope and belief. Justice Bridge recognized that for a drug addict like me the best thing would be a program that would allow me to spend some time behind bars and get treatment at the same time: the Work Ethic Camp program on McNeil Island. It was here in recovery that I started to believe in myself. It was here where I also had one of my first, powerful, spiritual awakenings. It came in a most peculiar way in a very unlikely location.

The story actually started when I was in the receiving unit at the Washington Corrections Center in Shelton. I had made friends with a guy who had been in prison for a while and still had a while to go. He and his cellmate were very "close" friends and I believe he might have been the "punk" as it were. The term "punk" has a vastly different definition in prison than it does on the fashion or music scene. Simply put, being a punk means you are someone's "bitch"—a sexual possession. This guy was friendly though, at least to me, but not in the way you are thinking. I think he and his overly muscled, thick-necked cellmate with the

Drugs, Food, Sex and *God*

oddly high voice were exclusive. One day, we were talking about the old days of doing drugs; I was talking about the old days, but he was actually talking about the past week. I was intrigued. How do you possibly shoot up meth in prison? Intrigued is an understatement. I was fascinated, enthralled, and completely enraptured by his story.

"No story, it is true," he said.

There is a certain amount of blind faith a person needs to buy drugs on the street. I hesitate to call it belief but it is blind nonetheless. You give your money to someone you don't know and then you pray he will come back. The odds are about 70/30. In prison, it is a different story, most likely because there is no money or street and the guy can't get very far away. One day my nice punk friend came up to me and handed me a baggie and a sock with something in it. I knew what was in the baggie so I didn't risk the sneak peak, but the sock was an enigma. I opened it up. Inside was an old-fashioned, glass syringe with a capped needle that may or may not have been new or sharp.

"You better wait till you get to McNeil before you use in case they piss-test you though," warned my friend.

Giddy with excitement I quickly walked back to my cell. I was running in my mind but I am certain I was walking so as not to call attention to myself. I sat in my cell with plans swimming in my head. My friend was absolutely right about waiting and I had a strong belief that if I had been caught with drugs in my system that I would not have been privileged to experience Justice Bridge's desire for my recovery. To hold these two ideas even in the same paragraph today makes me viscerally uncomfortable.

Chapter 3

I figured out a way of hiding the small baggie in the bottom of my deodorant. I figured my sneakiness trumped most correctional officers' doggedness. Besides if they used dogs then the deodorant might confuse them. The syringe was a different story. It was a beautiful antique-looking contraption that you might find in an apothecary shop in Mystic Seaport. I could not take the risk; I had to return this part of the gift.

As it turned out the transfer from Shelton to McNeil Island did not include drug-sniffing dogs, body cavity searches, urinalysis, or even much eye contact between guard and inmate. Actually, now that I was at Work Ethic Camp the guards were counselors and inmates were WECies (Work Ethic Camp Inmates). I got the lay of the land and settled in to my group. We were Group 72 and most of us were first-time offenders having done stupid things and had kind judges like my future friend, Justice Bridge. To be clear, we became friends long after this time in my life.

The baggie was melting a proverbial hole in my deodorant. I felt like the coast was clear. One day after some group activity, I was talking to one of my buds in Group 72 and intimated that I might have brought some "stuff" with me. He was as intrigued as I was with my friend back at Shelton. It kind of thrilled me to be such a bad boy and, in my mind, I fantasized that my new bud would want to fool around with the cool guy who got him high. Let's just say it had been a several-months-long dry spell on the sex front. Turns out that there is not as much man-on-man

Drugs, Food, Sex and *God*

sex going on in prison as you hear about, or at least there wasn't for me.

My new best friend and I went to the bathroom and took side-by-side stalls as I chopped up the meth from the baggie. I gave my friend a line on a little portable metal mirror under the stall wall and I could hear the faint mini vacuum sound as he took it in. I did my line and still had several left over. He declined a second and quickly left the bathroom. There I was with several lines of meth on a mirror in a bathroom stall in Work Ethic Camp on McNeil Island in prison on drug charges! It was as if God woke up inside me and realized what I was doing and screamed, "What the FUCK are you doing?"

There is no sound to a spiritual awakening. If there had been sound, it would have been a mammoth tree falling in the forest. With a blinding flash and thunderous reverberation, my downward spiraling life collapsed in on itself like a super nova or a black hole or whatever some huge galactic cataclysm is called. The journey I had set in motion to spiral to the bottom of my life had finally hit bottom and in a heartbeat had stopped flat, without an echo or a melody. Taking stock of my reality in this moment and making a split-second decision about my future yet to be, I quickly scraped the mirror's contents into the toilet, ripped up the baggie, and flushed my whole dark past into the prison's plumbing. I was free. Slowly the spiral started moving again, only this time the direction was upward.

I don't know if that is when I started to believe in God, but it could have been. I know that is when I stopped

Chapter 3

believing in the person I had become. In that instant, my whole life inverted. Black became white, down became up, and prison became freedom. My whole existence changed with a felled tree, with an awakening.

I don't know why certain dreams are so lucid. I imagine that dreams that come into the subconscious as your body is shutting down during an LSD overdose are SUPER real! It is hard to remember a cogent theme to each of these dreams but what I remember is that there were three distinct stories.

The first one was dark and frightening and there were tortuous struggles at every turn. The Pinhead guy from the *Hellraiser* movie was chasing me in a boat on a swamp. I have never even seen the movie so I really don't know how he got in there, but he was and maybe still is the boogieman. What I believe today is this is my dark, but necessary past. I don't think of it much, but when I do I am very grateful for it and its place in my life. Shutting the door on your past to ignore it is like shutting the screen door on the wind. It will blow right on through your life. It is better to recognize it for what it has been and be grateful for where it has blown you.

The second story in that night of dreams resulting from my LSD overdose in Hawaii starred me as a flight attendant. Not exactly sure why my subconscious picked flight attendant, except that I had just met Matthew who worked as one for United Airlines. Regardless of the reason, I was in service and I was trying to calm down the passengers, because we were crashing into a mountain. There was nothing to be done. I felt helpless, hopeless, and scared, yet others were looking to me for guidance, solace, and hope. As we crashed into the mountain suddenly everything inverted in color and feeling. Peace and overwhelming joy replaced fear and hopelessness. Even my brown and white uniform became white and brown including my black afro (I have no idea where the afro came from). The plane remained intact.

The peace that came over the passengers at the moment of crashing was much like that moment in the bathroom stall in prison. What I believe today is this is my life in service to others. Peace is what comes into the void left vacant when hopelessness goes. In that crash, I entered a life of service and a life I can believe in.

The third dream story was simply the book of my life with pages flipping backward. It was caught in a wind blowing right to left across its pages. I could plainly see each life point, each joy, each sorrow, as it flipped past. The crescendo was the slamming shut of the leather bound cover as it sat on a golden blanket in the antique cradle of my infancy. This is the dream of my life's purpose, my life's work to that point.

All three of these dreams ended abruptly in tune with the increasing voltage of the shocks applied to restart my heart in the ER. What I believe, and know with deep knowing and understanding, is that my purpose was not yet fulfilled and I was not ready to go. Today I can believe in God because of my dreams. I can believe in people because of others like Justice Bridge, and I can believe in myself because of my journey and my G.I.F.T.S.

CHAPTER 4:

Understanding Your G.I.F.T.S.

"Our deepest fear is not that we are inadequate. Our deepest fear is that we are powerful beyond measure. It is our light, not our darkness that most frightens us."
Marianne Williamson

To be gifted or given a gift is a special and amazing thing. Each of us is gifted in some miraculous way and many of us will always be searching for our gift. Finding it happens in the most spontaneous and unexpected ways.

I will never forget my first couple of college years. I was in a fraternity. I also was active in campus politics and was elected to the Board of Control for the Associated Students of the University of Washington. One of my duties as a BOC member was to be the liaison to the Ethnic Student Commissions. Me: white, from Republican roots, desperately trying to be straight, serving as a conduit for the needs of the ethnic students on campus. I was so far out of my comfort zone I radiated insecurity. Luckily for me there was Dorinda. Dorinda Henry was an activist and general "pot stirrer," as my mother would say.

On the surface of things, one could say that Dorinda was not nice, not remotely nice to me. But one needed to dig deeper to see that God had put Dorinda in my life for a reason. Clearly, that reason was to be the voice in the crowd that I truly needed to hear. At one particular meeting for something that seemed really important at the time, I was sitting on the stage and speaking into a microphone. I kept getting heckled and interrupted by some "pot stirrer" with a megaphone at the back of the crowd.

"George Baxter, why don't you come out of the closet?" said this militant black woman so that everyone could hear.

I tried to hold my composure and get through whatever it was I was trying to say but deep down I knew the voice was trying to preach something to me that was really important. I found the woman with the megaphone later and confronted her.

"What is your problem with me?" I asked.

"You are living a lie. It disgusts me to see you up there all preppy and shit, talking shit, and being shit when you are just full of shit."

Dorinda has a story all her own and has gone on to write about her life in a vulnerable memoir called *Bulldagger*. She has a gift of spotting truth and sharing that truth with everyone. Today she is Reverend Dorinda Henry and soon to be Doctor Reverend Dorinda Henry. She is a force to be reckoned with because of her gift, whether on a pulpit or with megaphone in hand. Her gift is truth.

Back in college I thought I hated her when in reality I really hated myself. Dorinda helped me to see that and to eventually be grateful for the man I have become. I never expected to ever see her again, but I was drawn to find out what had become of the militant dyke with the megaphone. She is using her superpowers for good in the world but she is still sharing her G.I.F.T.S. in some wonderful and unexpected ways.

It doesn't matter if you are black or white, male or female, straight or gay—there are certain aspects of your beingness that must be cataloged if you are to understand who you are. There is no particular order to these things but they conveniently spell G.I.F.T.S.: Gratitude, Insecurities, Foundational values, Threats to progress, and Spiritual truth. Take a specific and thorough inventory of these aspects of your life and you will truly know who you are and what makes you tick.

Gratitude

Like most aspects of life, Gratitude or the things we are grateful for, can be grouped into the Big Four major areas—Health, Wealth, Relationships, and Creative Expression. If you find yourself saying, "I have nothing to be grateful for in the area of health," for instance, you have to search harder. The same can be true for each of the other areas as well. If you look hard enough there is always something to be grateful for. It is in the essence and experience of gratitude that life changes. That life becomes LIFE. This is where all of the juiciness of recovery exists. Not everything looks like something to be grateful for. I have had a myriad of experiences and situations come up in my life where it is very hard for me to say I am grateful. But I am.

Health

I am grateful for Syphilis! There, I said it. Not that I wasn't equally grateful to get rid of syphilis, but I believe that the experience changed my life. The illness is treatable; however, let's just say that the treatment is a form of aversion therapy. Endure the treatment and eliminate the urge to repeat the behaviors leading up to the infection in the first place.

The bottom line is that I was acting like an addict with compulsive and obsessive sexual behaviors. I was putting myself in degrading and destructive situations from a health and a relationship perspective. Yes, I was actually in a relationship, although my behaviors were well outside social norms.

I had been involved in the most wonderful relationship, albeit platonic, with Bill. Turns out, Bill was and still is one of my best friends; but technically, we were "in" a relationship of a romantic nature.

This fact was not evident at dusk in Arboretum Park in Seattle. It is in the quiet, mysterious hours around dusk that the park comes alive with men, like me, lost in feelings of loneliness. We all were looking for a type of love that I didn't have in my relationship. I am quite certain that I did not admit my relationship status to anyone I spoke with that night, actually none of us spoke. There was just this unspoken dialog of looks and gestures that are the communication tools of the modern sex addict. This had taken the place left void by drugs and I used it the same

Chapter 4

way that I shot meth, without regard for my own or the public's safety. I am disgusted as I write this, but yet I am still grateful for this experience.

I knew as I sunk to my knees in the moist mud beneath the freeway on-ramps that something was not right. I knew it was wrong from start to finish and I thought it was my Episcopalian roots shooting up their tentacles of guilt into my psyche. I didn't realize at the time that I was being warned by a loving Universe to stop before it was too late. I did not stop.

Very soon after that, I began to feel fatigued only during half the day, and the chills and fevers were also intermittent. I went to see my doctor and he confirmed what deep inside I already knew. I had once again suffered the consequence of ignoring my inner voice. With my rear end aching from what seemed like gallons of penicillin injected into my muscles, I went home to sleep it off. Then death began to happen.

Syphilis is caused by a bacterium known as a spirochete. It causes minimal symptoms during its life cycle until it makes its way to the brain and then causes irreversible brain damage and insanity. As a side note, many of the great romantic writers and poets died of the insanity caused from the disease. This would not be my plight.

The life cycle can be arrested by our dear friend penicillin. In death, the contents of the spirochete are exhumed from within the cell and released to the host, me. "Holy God," I thought that death was my only relief. I had only felt that kind of horrific flu-like symptoms a couple of times in my life when I accidentally injected a random cotton fiber with my drugs causing what is lovingly referred to as "cotton fever."

During my tremors and massive sweat storm, I vowed to God and anyone who was listening (no one) that I was going to stop all of these behaviors and talk with Bill about our relationship and stop using this drug called sex.

Once again, a downward spiral collapsed. I knew it would not be an easy or delicate conversation, but it was absolutely necessary. That experience with the spirochete was the catalyst for the most honest conversation that Bill and I ever had. He is still one of my best friends today and there are no words to describe how grateful I am for that relationship.

My future depends on the care and compassion I have for my body temple. I can't continue to abuse myself with drugs. Nor can I act out compulsively with food or sex. The demands and declines are too great and it is the only vehicle I have to express what spirit has for me to express. I am so grateful for my health. I know that the truth of spirit in my life is perfect health and wellbeing.

WEALTH

It is impossible to really talk about wealth without a reference to money. Originally, I had such a powerful relationship around money that I wanted this book entitled "Money, Food, Sex, and God." Then I began to tell my story and realized that the story was primarily focused on drugs,

Chapter 4

not money; after God that is. I am so appreciative that my relationship with wealth, including money, is what it is.

I am not really sure what my relationship with money was early in life. Looking back, I am not really sure that I had a relationship, just that it was something I witnessed people wanting and through repeated exposure I wanted it too.

I would get an allowance each week. Money was so invisible to me that at the time I am not really sure what my allowance was or how much. I knew that if I wanted my allowance there were certain expectations placed on me; like loading the dishwasher and taking out the garbage.

I hated loading the dishwasher so I would purposefully do it incorrectly so I was given that chore less frequently. Incidentally, it was the same dishwasher that had the wooden top that I lit on fire. I really must have had some deep-rooted hatred for that dishwasher and what it represented to banish it to the fiery depths of hell.

Better than loading the dishwasher was taking out the garbage. The garbage was always at the end of the list of things to do because once I was outside I was not coming back in until "later." I was, I still am, distracted by bright shiny objects. I could answer the siren's call to climb a tree or play with a dead bird. I was free. Looking back on it, this freedom came from taking out the garbage, which was a chore I did to earn my allowance. I realized at a young age that there was a relationship between money from my allowance and freedom.

The thing about money I have come to realize is that left

unchecked it can make you crave more, like any addiction. At six or seven years old, I realized that I needed more money.

I didn't know why I needed money. There was never a lesson or class about jobs, investments, taxes, rent, vacations, cars, or buying food in elementary school. It should be taught in elementary school because beyond that people like me are not paying attention. Without a class like that, attention is not the only thing people like me are not paying.

I don't blame my parents for not properly teaching me about money. I have learned that I can't blame anyone. I just need to take personal responsibility. After all, I learned about sex on my own through trial and error; why not money too?

My first credit card was issued by the Bon Marché, now part of Macy's. The store was easily acquired by Macy's most likely because they gave too many irresponsible eighteen-year-olds credit cards. That credit card was also the first black mark on my credit report. At that age, I gave as much "attention" to that report as my third grade report card. I remember Ms. Bosnack said I would do better at school if I wasn't such a "social butterfly." Who says that about a child? Credit score, social butterfly, who could trifle with all this conjecture and judgment. I was having fun and needed to buy housewares.

I had a bit of a rocky start in my relationship with money. Every time I call it "a relationship," I giggle a little. I realize that it really was more of an arranged marriage. The picture I have is of two young children in some faraway land holding hands for the camera. The look on their faces is anything but joy. He is hoping that she doesn't turn into a dragon and swallow him whole and she wishes he didn't smell so bad.

If I had to pinpoint a time when the wheels truly fell off with my "lover" that was money it would have been in the early 1990s just after graduating from college. It was also just around the time I starting using drugs again. Not a coincidence that dysfunction follows drug use.

By the time I graduated with my Political Science degree from the University of Washington in 1990, I had not used drugs for about two and a half years. My once very active participation in a recovery community started to dwindle because of the time I was spending in school and other things that took priority over recovery. I also did not have enough time to cultivate friendships and I started feeling lonely. I was in a desperate pattern of work, school, homework, sleep, repeat. Looking back, I was losing my spiritual connection to my higher power. It was only a matter of time before I would find my life void and feel the need to fill that "God-Sized Hole" that had returned to the core of my being.

Without drugs holding a place in my life, I turned to one of my other distractions: sex. I discovered years earlier that sex was an easy way for me to make money but this night it was about feeling alone. A few hours at a sex club and I would no longer feel that loneliness was consuming me. I was not prepared for what God had in store for me on one particular night.

Standing in a towel, I met a man who looked as though he could single-handedly take away my loneliness and change my life, forever. I thought I had met my fairy-tale prince. He was in this den of sin looking very uncomfortable and out of place. I knew I needed to rescue him. How very wrong I was on all fronts, except one. My life was forever changed.

There are so many moments in my life that I would love to have just cried "victim" and blamed my circumstances on drugs like meth or alcohol. This night at the bathhouse was not one of those nights. I was sober. True, I was not using any substance. However, "sober" conjures a particular state of mind and I know now that my state of mind was impaired. The impairment was from addiction and the manifestation of that addiction was sex and then money. I soon discovered that this man oozed wealth and I was hooked.

Doing the same thing over again and expecting different results is a popular definition of insanity. Trying to end loneliness by walking around a sex club clad only in a towel never worked before and it was insane to think that this time would be different. However, I was insane.

This man was classy, nice clothes (once they went back on), nice car with a car phone. He was the first person I had met with a phone in the car. This, I thought, was the height of opulence and oh, how I was drawn to opulence.

He lived on Mercer Island, which at the time was one of the most affluent neighborhoods in the Seattle Metropolitan area. He owned his own business and was

Chapter 4

a hair stylist for some of the elite Seattle society. As time went on, he told me he loved me and asked me to marry him. He blinded me with a very expensive ring; I was still not using any substances but far from "sober."

Addiction specialists say that a person stops developing when they start using drugs and will stay frozen at that age until the substances go. Once that happens, the person can begin maturing again. I don't point this out in any way to excuse my blindness about this man. Emotionally though, I was about seventeen when we met. He was considerably older than that.

I was attracted to his relationship with money. I would say that I was attracted to his money, but he really didn't have any. I just made that up in my head. His cars were leased, he paid minimal rent on Mercer Island to some very good friends, and he went into debt buying my ring. He was a hairstylist and a good one. He did not own his salon but rather rented a chair in someone else's salon. He also liked to smoke pot. He was not a millionaire but lived like one; his relationship with money was to appear to have millions. Soon, we moved into a high-rise condo in downtown Seattle on the seventeenth floor looking out to Puget Sound—Heaven.

The first time I felt something amiss with money came through a conversation about his cell phone bill. Soon after he popped the question, I was driving his car and talking to one of my girlfriends about the proposal. I didn't know how long we talked and I didn't care. He did. He was considerably upset with how long I was on the call with my friend and was madly waving the car phone bill in my face pointing out how naïve and irresponsible I was. I immediately became that small boy again with the lump in my throat getting yelled at by my parents. I didn't grasp that money was not as "free flowing" as I had led myself to believe.

He helped me get a job teaching computer classes for one of his clients. She owned a freelance company that would contract with large businesses to begin teaching them how to use their corporate software. To put it in a time perspective, my first teaching assignment was teaching Windows 3.0. I appreciated him helping me start my career after graduating from university. The money was very good at $30-35 per hour. I was a great teacher, too, and could really make a very daunting subject easily accessible. The most important part was that I could contribute to our household expenses like food and rent.

I wasn't working a lot and would find myself back in that loneliness again, all alone in the apartment while he was at work. I would stare out at the ships coming into Elliott Bay wondering if this was it. I had alienated myself from most of my friends from recovery by spending all of my time with him. I was even tolerant of his smoking pot; after all, he was considerate enough not to smoke it in front of me. It wasn't long before isolation took me over.

Smoking pot became a good idea. I called an old friend who I knew would have some because I certainly wasn't going to smoke any that was in the apartment. I had not spoken with my friend in many years and misery always

Chapter 4

loves company so I was immediately invited to come over.

I remember that there was a basketball game on so chit-chat was kept to a minimum. Pleasantries were exchanged but we both knew why I was there so it wasn't some tearful homecoming between friends. He handed me a loaded bong and with a flick of the lighter, the life I was living changed. It was as if a secret door that had been closed for a long time suddenly opened and I was down the rabbit hole. I know what is meant when people say "one is too many and a thousand never enough."

It just took that one loaded bong to unravel my tightly wound up life. Looking back on it now, it needed unwinding. There was very little joy brightening my home life. I thought that I had met the man of my dreams but it turns out that it was really more of a house of cards and once I started using drugs again I was more inclined to just knock the whole thing over. I realized that the relationship this man had with money was very superficial and most of it was to look a particular way to a particular group. Having the cute young boyfriend helped complete that picture. Turns out it was not a fit for me.

Within the space of a month, I had started putting together my own new life, on paper. I purchased a Mercedes and bought a condo on Queen Anne Hill, two symbols of wealth that I figured would signify a better relationship with money. Honestly, the Mercedes was fourteen years old and the condo was a "rent to own" on the back side of the hill in the "lower rent district." But the truth and the telling of the truth don't always have to be perfectly matched especially when you are back doing drugs.

Drugs, Food, Sex and *God*

I was still teaching computer classes and was making better money than I had ever made in my life. I was self-employed and had my own business as Baxter & Associates. It was a vague business name so I could use it for any number of business ventures. The problem with being self-employed is this thing called self-employment tax that takes an extra 15 percent off everything that you make. No one really tells you that when you go off on your own. When you make a bunch of money and you do drugs you really are signing up for paycheck-to-paycheck living; paying taxes doesn't fit into that picture. If my house of cards had a shaky foundation, I would have to say it was due to drugs and taxes. After all these were the only two things for sure in my life; even death was eluding me. My behaviors demonstrated what could have easily been called a "death wish."

In the spring of 1991, I moved part-time into the woods to set up a camp in Index, Washington. It was specifically a Gay Camp, one of my favorite redundant phrases. For people like me, it was an excuse to party all the time and run around the woods naked.

The constraints of the camp were pretty clear. In order to keep it for the summer, I would have to occupy it at least one or two nights a week. Living up there full-time became the thing to do and everyone who came up just on weekends was an interloper.

I wish I could say I was saving money by living up there, but I still had my condo in the city. My drug use had ramped up. I remember at one point, I took LSD every

Chapter 4

night for eighteen nights straight. Most days I would make the ninety-minute drive to Tacoma to teach computer lessons to the managers of Pacific Northwest Bank. What I would give to have a video tape of any one of those lessons. Driving sleep-deprived while coming down off LSD is consistent with having a death wish. Working sleep-deprived coming down off LSD is the closest thing I had to a work ethic at the time.

Can you imagine if one of your workshop teachers or college professors showed up every day high on LSD? The feedback I got from those classes was quite positive. In fact, they kept me on and sent me to continue the classes in Spokane, which is a chapter for another day. Let's just say that was the week I found out what Cross Tops were: pharmaceutical speed.

From a money standpoint, I realized sometime that summer in the middle of an LSD trip that the only way I would get ahead financially was if I stopped working at jobs that could be taxed, and focused on a different source of income. I started looking at my options, which included, not in any particular order, prostitution, drug dealing, and a paper route under the table for my friend who was having a nervous breakdown and couldn't drive. It is amazing how therapeutic it is to throw newspapers at the front doors of houses and get paid for it.

I have always had an ability to manifest things, situations, and people in my life. It wasn't long before my desire for non-taxable employment outweighed my desire for a legitimate job and I devised a way to get fired from my computer-teaching job. Writing it this way makes it sound as though it were difficult to get fired. It was, in actuality, quite simple. I only had to no-show three times when my boss was really counting on me. Come to think about it, not showing up for work three times in two weeks was working pretty hard to get fired. I would have fired myself after the second time and felt completely justified.

Before long, I had three new careers: paperboy, escort, and drug dealer. I knew that I could use the money I made with these new tax-free careers to pay the tax bill from the last career. By the time I settled that tax bill it was over $30,000 in taxes and penalties. Let's just say that the past experience I had with the IRS gave me a new appreciation for the tenacity of our government.

I am not feeling compelled to use this chapter about wealth to go into details about my paper route, escort business, or the drug dealing. I am quite certain that each of these will come out in vivid detail in other chapters. Perhaps it is just this author's way of ensuring that you will keep reading this book. I know how hungry some of you are for the details.

This section is about money and how my early dysfunctional relationship with it needed to be addressed for me to move on. I would like to report that all of my debts are paid and I am consistently saving money and spending it wisely on things that I have carefully considered before purchasing, but that still would not be true. It has gotten much better because it has gotten much more conscious.

My relationship with money has transcended the

day-to-day commerce with cash, check, or charge. I am no longer controlled by my old messages of scarcity and lack, and know that money is merely a tool that I use to relate with the world. Wealth is a broader context of generosity both of spirit and of resources. Sharing wealth today is the act of giving oneself through time, talent, and treasure—the three Ts.

I remember hearing the word "tithing" growing up in the Episcopal/Methodist Church. I did not really relate it to a specific giving ritual. I had no idea about its roots or its meaning. "Tithe" quite simply means "a tenth" and comes from Old English. Commonly, what it means is to give a tenth or set aside a tenth. Think about a farmer for instance. A farmer plants a full field of a crop and the field is full and lush with bounty. If that same farmer sells everything, that farmer will be wealthy in the short term, but will have nothing left to plant the following year. If that same farmer sets aside a tenth of the harvest for seeds for next year, then he or she is almost as wealthy from the sale of 90 percent of the crops and has a bounty each and every year.

Today, I use this same analogy to give of my time, talent, and treasure. This is how I spiritually "seed" my future harvest. It is really easy. The challenge is to decide where you set it aside. For me, I have chosen places where I am spiritually fed and the decision about where is very personal. The mechanics are what I wish to discuss. The money piece is a "no-brainer"—get a hundred, give or set aside ten. You can get into a discussion about gross or net, but those are also very personal decisions about defining what you think is "yours." I want my future to be seeded by the tithe of my gross. Where the mechanics become challenging is in regards to talent and time.

I still have not figured out how to parse out 10 percent of my talent and give it away. I am not completely sure what all of my talents are actually. Still today, I find that I can completely discount a large portion of my talent and think that I have no talent at all, but that is actually the topic of the chapter on Inventory of G.I.F.T.S.

Time is easy like money. You can give from net or gross. I give of my time in meditation, which includes daydreaming (covered in the chapter on Dreaming). I used to try to figure out the time I needed to spend in net hours in the day, twenty-four hours minus sleep hours. I found that I was always trying to figure out if I slept seven hours or six hours and if I needed to meditate for one hour and forty-two minutes or forty-eight minutes. What a bother. I spent more "time" trying to figure out where to set aside my time than I did actually setting it aside. Two hours and twenty-four minutes is what I set aside every day for meditation, contemplation, and reflection. Because I am human, I am rarely perfect nor exact, but it is the consciousness that I place in this relationship with time where the healing can take place.

In my healing, I find that I do have a new relationship forming with money as well. There are still those old ideas that creep into this relationship but overall things are getting better. The most important part of any relationship in the Big Four is about consciousness. My consciousness around wealth has greatly deepened. It is no longer some invisible thing that is unattainable to a small boy or some menacing force ready to pounce at the slightest inkling of increase. I no longer have to deal on the black market to make money and keep my wealth safe. Today, out in the open, I can express my wealth through my life choices in ways that transcend greed and opulence but that acknowledge my family, my community, my world, and me.

One of the most memorable opportunities to practice the notion of wealth was a trip that Travis and I took to Cambodia in 2013. We went with a group from our spiritual center or we probably would never have gone. Cambodia was not really on either of our bucket lists.

The trip was not extravagant by any means but did include the obligatory day at Angkor Wat and the other temples seen in the *Tomb Raider* movies. Prior to leaving, however, my beauty and wellness business, Seattle Youthful, had a very good quarter and we were able to extend our generosity in ways that we had not been able to in the past. We have found that the simple act of conscious giving has immeasurable ramifications in our life and connects us with the world in untold ways.

We used some of our windfall to purchase a well for a family in Cambodia without knowing at the time the impact that this would have. It wasn't until we were in the country standing in the backyard of this family's home that the impact was truly felt.

I walked out into a lush vegetable garden careful not to

step outside the neat walking rows; my feet were much bigger than the path. The ground beneath was hard-packed, dry, and lifeless. I heard the gleeful peal of laughter from a small boy as he pumped the handle on this well at the edge of the garden and it hit me. This was lifeless land like the path that I was walking on before the life that was brought forth with this water. This family was feeding themselves and their neighbors with the food from this garden. The children of this family and neighboring families may be able to concentrate just a little better in their school day without the grip of hunger that may have been present before the well. Emotion hit me like a freight train and there in the middle of this Eden in the rural farmland around Siem Reap, I wept uncontrollably. I realized at that moment that this was not some $400 gift to the disadvantaged who were faceless and unseen. This was life pumping up from the earth that was not there before because I had been healed of the old messages of lack, limitation, and scarcity. This was not invisible wealth but very visible, tangible, palpable, and delicious. That was the sweetest tasting water I had ever consumed. I allowed myself to weep and to feel the full-throated emotion of this experience. Travis's life and mine were forever changed in that moment and I realized that I had a responsibility as Gandhi put it "to be the change I want to see in the world."

I am not suggesting that everyone buy a well in Cambodia. I am suggesting that there are things each of us can do to change the consciousness around wealth in our world. It is not always the big philanthropic things either. Sometimes it is just the simple things that have the greatest impact.

Chapter 4

Here is a simple idea that I put to action. When I go to the Starbucks near my work to buy my coffee, I pay for one additional Grande Drip coffee. I tell the barista that the next person who orders a Grande Drip should receive the additional cup I purchased and to tell them that someone bought it for them. It is a kind of "paying it forward" that always makes me feel good about my day.

Today, I am becoming the person I always dreamed of being. I remember being a young boy and having an image in my head of the man I would be someday. I lost my way and went off the path for a little while in life, but it was through all of the experiences that I have had that I am the person I am today.

Relationships

Relationships are a vital part of what makes us human beings. There is a spiritual connection that happens for people as they bond together in community. Throughout my life, I have formed bonds with many people who today I consider among my friends, but there only is one first best friend. For me that was Tiny. That was not her name but it is what I called her.

Tiny was very cool and I remember being in awe of her life from a very early age. Her mother was an oil painter and her father head of the math department at a major New York University. I remember wishing that I had a normal family like hers. I would walk into her house and there was always an unfinished nude woman on the canvas fixed to an easel. I had no fascination with the nudity but instead was enthralled with the intricacy of the brush strokes. A young boy not into paintings of nude women … red flag. I can still conjure up the wonderful olfactory pleasure that oil paint mixed with linseed oil has for me though.

Tiny and I were basically inseparable. Every day I would wait for her to come home from her private school so we could play. I always thought it was cool that she went to a private school and not to Main Street Elementary School like me. She went to Harbor Country Day School, which sounded like a spa for young minds.

Tiny had a horse named Compact that she would ride in horse shows. She was quite good, I think. She had a lot of ribbons, regardless. I got to be Compact's groomer and loved to brush his silky coat. I loved being around horses, and horse people seemed so exciting.

Tiny and I did almost everything together that young children do. She was a year and a half older than I was but it never mattered much. Tiny taught me how to be a friend. We fought likes kids do; screamed "pig" and "dummy" at each other across the front yard, but she taught me how to be loyal and thoughtful and to always have each other's back if there was trouble. Sometimes there was trouble.

One warm autumn afternoon we were up exploring near one of the neighbor's houses. Tiny and I lived next to each other on Van Brunt Manor Road but behind our houses was a newer housing development with bigger houses without the pleasure of waterfront, like ours. What they did have, though, at this particular house was a fishpond.

Chapter 4

The house was owned by a child psychologist who both of us remember was not very nice to anyone, including children. He never had Halloween candy, ever.

The fishpond was a world unto itself. We were mesmerized and fascinated by the doctor's fish. It seemed like there were hundreds of them in different shapes and sizes. There were so many that they were pretty easy to catch. We played "fisherpeople" for hours after school and made sure to be gone before Doc would get home from his important job.

It is unclear whose idea it was that day to take a couple of fish, but I think it was probably mine. I had a reputation for being kind of sneaky and with all of those fish, how could he miss two little ones.

The Great Fish Heist of 1971 was perfect in its planning and execution. We brought baggies with us like they give at the actual fish store and some bread ties to close them up with. We sat up at the pond and ate Halloween candy from the previous week's haul, no thanks to the doctor.

So many colors, shapes, and sizes. I can't remember what Tiny chose for her new friend but I carefully selected a black goldfish with big bulging eyes like a hammerhead shark. It might as well have been a shark though because I was not clear how I would ever get it in my house past the watchful eye of Carol Baxter. Then it hit me: The Perfect Plan!

I arrived confidently at the front door of my house greeted by my mother. "Where did that hideous fish come from?" bellowed my mom.

"Tiny's mom bought it for me at the pet store. Isn't it

wonderful?" I said, quite proud of myself. At that exact moment, the same story was being related by Tiny making my mother out to be some-kind-of-wonderful.

My first foray into illegal activity seemingly was quite successful until there was a knock on the front door that evening. It was the doctor. Apparently, we were not very tidy with our candy debris and our cover was foiled by the evidence of mini Hershey Bar wrappers. The child psychologist was incredulous that two children could be so cunning and mischievous. He was clearly undone by the whole affair and we were forced to return the fish and apologize. We promised to never go back to the pond again and we never did.

When we moved to Seattle from Long Island in 1978, I lost touch with Tiny. I was all caught up with making new friends and trying to figure out the way to make them like me. All other friends were compared to Tiny—my first best friend—either consciously or unconsciously. I never saw her again, but thought about her all of the time. The funny thing about consciousness and connection is that we communicate and are connected in ways that we have yet to understand. I was working on this part of my story just the other day, when I received a Facebook message from Tiny—after more than thirty-three years!

Creative Expression

Sometimes creative expression does show up, like your profession. I was born to be a nurse. I am sure of it. I love

Chapter 4

the creativity I can offer life itself as I work and have my being as a nursing professional. I learned many of my skills as a nurse during my dark years, if you can believe it. There is no time that was as clear as one night in the Emergency Department.

If you have ever been in a hospital ER, you will agree that they are anything but quiet and restful. There is a constant barrage of noise and alarms, mostly unimportant. As an ED nurse, I tended to tune out most of the noise, but I needed to quickly sort the not-so-important from the super important among the beeps and bings.

All ED nurses are installed with an internal sensor for important noises and smells. Thankfully, there is also a filter that was installed by the "manufacturer" (our human biology) that makes unremarkable the smells of booze, poop, urine, and puke. This one day my internal sensor was going off and called me into the room of my next patient. A six-year-old Hispanic boy I will call Javier had fevers that his mother had been caring for at home for a week. From her very scattered English I understood he had been doing okay at home, but recently became worse and lethargic so she brought him in.

I came back into the room and looked at her panicked face and looked at my patient. Something was changing and my sensor said, "Spring into action, NOW!"

Without even skipping a beat I pulled up the IV start cart and started to place an IV in the young boy's hand while giving a calm look to the mother as if to say, "I will do everything I can for your boy; he is in my hands." Just as I started to put in the IV needle, he went into febrile seizures and I knew that I needed to trust my skills at finding a vein on this very sick boy.

I was instantly transported back ten years when I was trying desperately to find a vein on another very sick boy. Me. My arms showed all the telltale signs of a desperate junkie with shaky hands. I just wanted to get high, get normal, get "well." I remember the false starts and the burning pain as I would ravage my body with toxic chemicals compounded into methamphetamines. Over and over, I would try in a fevered pitch with sweat pouring off my forehead and stinging my sunken eyes, my soul dimming more and more with each fatal attempt.

All at once, I would get that flash of red in the needle. The sense of relief even before pushing in the plunger can only be characterized by descriptions of Nirvana. I knew my version of "wellness" was on the way.

I had that same rush of relief, now, when I was able to get Javier's IV in while he was thrashing in a seizure. I knew that I could now help save his life and break his seizure. His mother looked at the relief on my face and knew in an instant that I had the gift that was going to save her son's life. Luckily, she had no idea where I had gotten my gift.

Apparently, I did well in the school of hard knocks and I can be grateful in that moment that I went through those experiences years ago. I learned about vascular anatomy and got over my fear of needles the hard and painful way. It was like that quite often in the ED. My peers knew that I had mad IV skills. Some knew how I had come upon

Chapter 4

them and some were just awed by watching me put the IV catheters in places where they did not even know there were veins, grateful that I knew.

INSECURITIES

I have this habit of disclosing too much, too soon, and too often. You would never have guessed this by reading the cover of this book! I don't know how many first conversations I have had where somehow my biggest, darkest secrets came out. I guess I have trained myself to get it all out on the first conversation because with behavior like that there is seldom a second, which seems like a strange catch-22.

It is like dating. I have a friend who was diagnosed with herpes simplex virus and it impacts her dating. "When should I disclose that?" she would ask me, like I am the best person to ask for dating advice. My advice, "Hi, nice to meet you, I have HSV; my name is Susie." Clearly, not the best intro but it does get the deal-breakers on the table. I believe that if you get it all out quickly then people can make the determination if they want you in their life or not.

It makes me an open book and shows a level of honesty not frequently found. At least that is what I tell myself. What about a little mystery? Sometimes the only action needed is inaction. What if I just listened when I wanted to talk about myself? Would that make me seem less self-absorbed and less insecure? Really that is my goal, show up and be confident.

Why is it then in a quest for confidence that I let some of my most outrageous insecurities see the light of day? For me, it is about power. Not making myself more powerful but taking the power out of the insecurities.

When I was younger, I would find a way to work into the conversation about my sexual preference. That way my new acquaintance couldn't find out about it later and try to hurt me with the information. To varying degrees, I still do that with my insecurities in an attempt to take away the power they hold over me.

Most of my insecurities today boil down to fear or unworthiness. Either way, they tend to belong to an untrue story that I perpetually tell myself in an attempt to derail my life. I am not sure how this derailment might lead to me feeling more secure but it might go something like a self-fulfilling prophecy.

Let's take my fear of educational failure, for instance. It was never as apparent as it was in my doctoral program. From day one, I had a sense of rampant fraud. I felt so overwhelmed.

I remember sitting in class the first day of orientation. I felt like David at a Goliath Convention. There were major nursing powerhouses from all over the country in the room. I felt "less than." I felt that the admissions committee had made a horrible and embarrassing mistake and decided, as a huge joke, they would throw some silly inexperienced nursing hick from Seattle into the mix.

From that day on, I decided that I was not going to be the butt of some elitist joke. I went into overachiever mode.

Chapter 4

Insecurity led to achieving, even though every semester I thought about dropping out. Funny thing is that every one of my classmates felt the same way at some point in the program. Each of us felt like we did not belong there, even the most accomplished nurse in the room. I started the quest for a reality check with a simple question that many of us would echo throughout the halls of the nursing building, "You know what they call the person at the bottom of our class?"

"Doctor," we would all gleefully reply and that was the truth. The truth was that I was not in the bottom of my class, and was selected as the convocation speaker for our final graduation ceremony.

Most insecurity is not real. It is a movie we create in our head. Left to our own devices, we do not tend to create a love story and usually the movie is some horror film or a Sci-Fi thriller where something unexplainable is trying to turn us inside out. Insecurity is a perversion of the truth, a perception that has been convoluted by childhood psychoses and bears no resemblance to the way things really are. To get a true understanding of those things that make you insecure ask yourself, "What does the evidence show?" If you want to know how you believe, look at your life. If you don't have the life that you want, then change what you believe about the life you have.

I have come to the conclusion that it is not rational to look back on my life and witness what I have overcome, experience joy upon joy and success after success, and still feel like a failure. What is rational is that there is something wrong with my perception of myself. I have a belief about myself that needs to change and that work needs to happen within me. This is why this inventory of insecurities is important. It leads us to do the internal work of changing the beliefs that we have about ourselves and how we see the world. It takes away the blame of the outside world and puts the choice of personal responsibility in our lap where it belongs. Today I am enough.

Foundational Values

Foundation: strong, firm, stable from which to build upon. It's funny because until I started writing this section on G.I.F.T.S., I rarely consciously thought about what my foundational values were. When I think of foundation, I am immediately drawn to the thought of the houses and places where I have lived in my life.

On Long Island, our house had a basement that felt like a bomb shelter. It was thick-walled and smelled earthy and moist. The only crack that I remember in this foundation was at the bottom of the stairwell down from the kitchen. The crack was made when my head came in contact with the cement at the base of the stairs after a headfirst transit from top to bottom. I am not sure but that could have been where all of my problems began or perhaps it is just a convenient excuse. "Oh, that's just George. He fell down the stairs and hit his head as a boy. Ain't never been right since."

We moved to Vashon to a two-story split-level built on

Chapter 4

a solid slab foundation. It was stable but pretty uninspiring. The only thing I remember was that it was signed by "Werner" with a stick in cement like a piece of art. I hope that Werner didn't give up his day job to pursue an art career.

During my stint up in the woods of Index, Washington living in a tent, the foundation was made of wood and flimsy by any foundation standards. The floor was uneven, but essentially served its only purpose, which was to keep me from sleeping in the mud.

My current house is built on a solid foundation. Its only purpose is to protect the infrastructure and keep a very substantial house solid and standing. I imagine that the foundation is just as strong as the structure built upon it. It is new and modern with protection from flood, fire, and quake. The type of foundation that will be here long after its purpose has been served.

These four literal foundations represent the transition of my personal foundational values. I was raised in a family with deep, strong, stationary, unmovable values. I was born into these values and accepted them as my very own, even if I banged my head into them from time to time. My family was and still is very conservative. There are many aspects of my life that significantly challenge the values of the lives of my family. They have always held strong to these values and, whether I agree or not, there is something remarkable about their consistency to hold strong. I want to think that it was this consistency that led to my father not attending my wedding to Travis. Any other reason just simply hurts too much.

During my high school and college years, I am not sure what my foundational values were. I was so into recreational drugs and drinking that my values changed with regularity. Isn't it nice to call it recreational drug use? I guess it is a recreation until you make a career out of it.

When I was deep in my career drug use, I can't say that my values were any more supportive than the wood platform at Index. My values at the time just barely kept me from sleeping in the mud. I held fast to the notion that I needed to stay one step ahead of everyone and everything because "they" were all out to get me.

Paranoia had become a foundational value along with fear, hate, and more self-loathing. I thought briefly about suicide. In my relationship with God at the time, I felt suicide was the only sin. This was my singular life-saving value in the midst of what my life had become. That one value kept me alive long enough to change my values, my life, and my idea of sin.

Today, my values are simple, strong, and positive. I hold fast to the value that the only sin is a feeling of separation from God. I know that the Universe conspires for my unlimited joy and benefit, and that people are inherently good. People still can do horrible things to each other and to themselves but I believe this comes from that feeling of separation from a Universal Power that propels us forward as a people.

Today, I take inventory constantly of my foundational values. I consider each day how my choices match up to how I believe. When there are inconsistencies, I take corrective action or amend the wrong. In Twelve Step recovery terms, this is called a daily tenth step, and I know that it keeps me connected with the Universal power by staying right with my values.

Threats to Progress

Threats to progress are simply those things in your life that transcend irrational insecurities and could actually derail your whole life. For some it could be some psychological threat like an abuser who might come back in your life and stir up the old issues, problems, and pain. For others it may be something more physical like illness or an accident.

Threats can mask themselves in many disguises and this is why it is critical that you take inventory of anything that you know could derail your life and progress. The obvious threat for me in my life is using drugs again. Don't get me wrong; my life is fantastic and using is way off my radar; however, it has happened before.

I will never forget a particular time I was walking down a trail at that gay campground in Index, Washington. I was high. Probably methamphetamines. I know that it was not alcohol because I had not yet given up being "sober." I had this wildly perverted notion that alcohol was my problem previously and all other substances I could control.

This day, though, I was walking down this trail with a wonderful lesbian woman who regularly camped there. She told me that she was sober and attended AA meetings. I don't remember why the conversation was so emotional for me, but I broke down in tears to this woman and told her I had to get back to a program of recovery. I told her that I had been sober for two and a half years and those had been some of the most special and wonderful years of my life. The tears were deep, mournful, full of anguish, and remorse and in that conversation, I was able to reflect on my life, my recovery and my relapse, and pain.

I was active in a recovery program, really active. The type of program doesn't matter. At the time, it was what I needed. I had a sponsor and went to meetings daily. I was doing service and there was nothing, nothing that could get in the way of my recovery. I did steps and took inventory of my life and my resentments. I thought I had done a very thorough job on my inventory. But I had not looked at those things that could threaten my recovery at all. I just shut them out as though there was no way they could possibly happen.

My relapse started long before I used any other substances. It started when I moved back to Seattle in 1990 away from my support network in Los Angeles. I went back to school and was more focused on classes than meetings, and I did not have the time to spend doing service work. Then I got into a relationship that was very hot, quick, and heavy with a great deal of emotional angst and heavy marijuana use.

It did not take much to lead me from a path of recovery back into the depths of using substances to deal with my feelings about school, the relationship, the end of the relationship, and the ensuing loneliness—the biggest threat of all. I would do anything to keep from feeling lonely, and still will. I am not afraid to admit it; in fact, it is more dangerous for me to keep that threat to myself. Isolation is the darkroom where I develop my negatives.

I started hanging out with the wrong crowd at the wrong places. Most of my friends were people I met at the bar or the bathhouse. They were my people now, the people who kept me from my loneliness. I would go anywhere they went and do anything they would do, almost. I drew the line at drinking again or using needles. I drew the line and redrew the line until there really was no line. The biggest threat was crossing the line at all and it still is. Sometimes all I have to keep me on the right side of the line and to keep me from the abyss of loneliness is my faith in God. Luckily, today that is enough.

I wish I could say that the only threat to me today is using drugs. Substances like alcohol, pot, meth, and cocaine are not the only things that can lead me on a path of hopelessness, helplessness, despair, and degradation. It actually is all forms of addiction. Drugs, food, and sex are all the ways I've used to hurt myself in the past and are all threats to my progress today. And, with one of those addictions, I must find my way because I have to consume it every day: Food.

There has to be some awareness that my behaviors are out of check when I have gone back to the toaster for my third pair of "emotional slices." Yeah, I know that there is absolutely nothing in Dave's Killer Bread that can quiet emotions like fear or unworthiness, but there I am hovered over the toaster like a hobo over a fifty-five gallon drum fire.

The bread is low-carb bread but it really doesn't matter when you are going for slice number six. Waiting for the toast to pop I butter an untoasted piece just to tide me over. STOP! What am I feeling? Fear, loneliness, anger, resentment, uncomfortable joy, overwhelming happiness?

No, it was just a Tuesday. Why was I was acting out? It really wasn't the true me, it was my little self, ego. I wanted what I wanted and I wanted more of it. This was my pattern with drugs too. I just could not do a little social methamphetamine, recreational crack, or lunchtime LSD. When I give in to self-will, I am a pig. There is nothing but the dismal illumination of past traumatic remorse that I am left with, promising to never do it again.

At least at the toaster I still have a chance for survival. It is not drugs that are killing me. My behaviors can have damaging and lasting effects like my abdominal spare tire that I am sure is filled with cinnamon toast crunch cereal. I laugh about it now because I don't have these moments very often. The reason they don't happen like they did in the past is because of inventories like this one.

My triggers center in drugs, food, and sex. There have been so many sexual experiences that left me so hopeless and empty that there are times I just thought ending my life was the only solution. I won't go into detail, because it is unnecessary and too painful to write. I hope you aren't disappointed about the lack of salacious and depraved details of an addict acting out sexually. You'll have to buy my "historical" novel called "Fifty Shades of Gay" (not coming to a bookstore near you).

We all have our triggers. Perhaps you are addicted to Internet porn. Maybe you have problems with anger or fidelity or stealing. Whatever your issues and triggers are, it is critical to make them known, maybe not to the world like the one I have, but known at least to you. Take inventory and make friends with those things that could stop your progress in life. If you really want to change and want a better life, commit to finding out what needs changing.

Spiritual Truths

I remember when it hit me that I needed a deeper spiritual relationship with something, anything actually. After all, I was continuing to go through this internal battle about acting out sexually whether it was at the bathhouses or parks. It was a Monday morning and I had stayed out particularly late the night before doing "God knows what." I was hung over but not in the traditional sense of the word. I hope by now a few things are particularly clear.

First is that I do not use drugs, including alcohol, anymore and second, from an addiction standpoint, that matters very little. It matters a lot if you are struggling to stop using drugs because that is the biggest surrender necessary for addicted people. However, when it comes to feelings of helplessness, hopelessness, degradation, and dereliction, it is the power of addiction that is at play. The particular substance really doesn't matter. For me, food and sex provide all of the spiritual void I required at this point. And there it is.

Spiritual void means lacking in the awareness, understanding, and acceptance of a spirit greater than my ego in my life. The solution would be for me to deepen my relationship with my higher power. A good and reasonable starting point might be the appropriate use of capitalization. Higher Power and God. Is that so difficult? I had gotten it in my lexicon that I would no longer be capitalizing those words but I have even gone so far as to cross out when, God forbid, I accidentally used capital G or capital H.P. Clearly, something needed to change.

Monday morning, in my car, driving to a job I really hated. "Okay, God," I said to no one and nothing in particular. "If I am supposed to have some belief in you or Jesus Christ or whatever, you are seriously going to have to show me the right way and don't be subtle because I clearly do not know how to do this on my own."

This conversation with God began what I lovingly refer to as "The Search for Church." I started an active and intentional search for my spiritual home. What happened from that intentionality is beautiful in its unfolding.

The very first thing that I noticed, besides a sense of peace, was that I did not feel like throwing up when I got to my job at the cardiology office. I no longer had the attachment of having to make this arrangement and job fit for me. I was free and at peace with all of it.

The search for church was leading me in many directions seemingly all at once. I had my intention set on finding a spiritual home and I was trying out different plans of action looking for the one that would be a perfect fit. After all, finding the right spiritual center was not something that could be methodically planned out. One must trust in … I don't know, God, maybe.

I remember one week sitting in this big church in the New Thought Movement and thinking, "I could be at home here." There always seemed to be a "but" that followed that thought.

I tried the Lutheran Church because one of my many attempts at finding Mr. Right was Lutheran. He also lived in Minneapolis and was a Sex Addict; it's actually how we met. Not really "Mr. Right" material, looking back on it, but I was desperate for connection.

I also went back to my Episcopal roots and attended, twice, St. Mark's Cathedral. The second time was a confirmation of the first. Funny thing is I think I was confirmed at St. Mark's. This confirmation was that it was not my Church Home.

Home is warm and inviting, welcoming of family and friends. Home has a quality of being that is undefinable in words but feels absolutely right when you are there. When you walk into your home you feel wrapped up in a safe, warm blanket of goodness that almost feels like gravy topping a steak. My friend Sherrie calls this "Love Gravy" and it doesn't even sound dirty when she says it.

I was back to the New Thought community. I don't know what pulled me or called me there, but it was a way of being that resonated for me. God is in everything and does not need to be coerced to help you or anyone! God is in this pen and this ink and my thoughts as I write. There is no getting away from this God. I like that. I was very comfortable with the messenger too. The senior minister had a message that I enjoyed, although I had no connection with her in person. She had virtual celebrity status and I was on the outside looking in, a place for which I alone am responsible.

While I half-heartedly decided this would be my church, I found myself attending infrequently. I also hoped to find my mate in a spiritual community like this. God had a similar plan only slightly different, typically God. When I met my husband, Travis, he wanted a spiritual community also and we started attending weekly together.

The church had awesome music and we were frequently moved to tears by the inspiration of it. One artist in particular named Jami Lula drew us into his musical world of God and Spirit and we could not get enough Jami. That day in church, we purchased all of his albums and found out that he was giving a concert the following Friday night at a church named Genesis. This church was a mere seven minutes from our house. Our current church was a good forty-five minute drive each way.

We went to the concert and saw some friends we knew from our recovery community. The church had a fun, homey feel and we felt welcomed by everyone. We were invited to try it out that Sunday because Jami would be performing at the Sunday service as well. If Jami would be there then so would we; however, there was no way we would be giving up our other church.

Something happened that Sunday in July 2011 that defies

Chapter 4

definition. We came home. The warmth and security we felt as we were ushered into that community that day was like nothing either Travis or I had ever felt in any spiritual community. I knew in an instant that spirit had answered my prayer, yet again.

All of that seems so long ago. Since that day, Travis and I were married in that church and both of us serve the community with absolute joy. We study the teachings and deepen our understanding of what it is to live with intention and love.

The transformation of our lives has been astounding as we have opened our hearts to that sense of wholeness that is found in our spiritual center. I take inventory every day with profound spiritual practice.

Spiritual giants never declare their gigantism, like Homer Simpson, for instance. Never has he said, "Marge, I am a spiritual dynamo. God exists in my very essence." Just because he has never said it doesn't mean that it isn't true. More about Homer in a minute.

I have had an abundance of definitions of God and my spiritual center both before prison and after. Before prison, my spirituality centered mostly on me in some egocentric, holier-than-thou, look-at-me-I-might-be-the-reincarnation-of-Jesus sort of way. Now many years later I realize that all of my definitions and descriptions of God had one thing in common: me.

Take my Homer Simpson version of God, for instance. I see God, Spirit, Higher Power, whatever, as a big pink donut that follows Homer Simpson around. Floating in the air behind Homer, it goes everywhere he goes. A big, fat-filled, yummy, sugary, monolith of goodness that is, in essence, God to Homer. Now, imagine that the only thing that Homer needed to do to suck out the fatty goodness from this inexhaustible supply was stick in a straw and suck. How often would Homer stick in that straw? Just in the morning? Maybe three to four times a day?

What I am referring to is called "conscious contact." Homer Simpson, with all of his foibles would have his straw in 24/7 sucking all the goodness out of that pink donut. The worship that Homer has with food, especially sugary foods, is clearly not how I want my diet to go; however, I am talking about conscious contact with God.

God is always there with yummy deliciousness and always available and never exhausted. The only question is when and why do I stop sucking on the straw?

Imagine if we had that kind of singleness of purpose that Homer Simpson has. "Seek ye first the kingdom of Heaven and all else will be added unto you." Except we don't seek heaven first and by heaven I mean joy, beauty, abundance, freedom, life. We get too caught up in the right job and enough money and gossip. It is too easy without a ritual to lose sight of the most important things and get lost in the mire of mediocrity without a spiritual center.

Worship is that focused attention that we pay out like currency every day. It doesn't matter if it is "good" for you or "bad." The spiral can go both ways, remember. I don't know when I consciously stopped sucking the fat from my God donut and used the straw to worship a different God but I did. I worshiped the drugs, degradation, and depravity. Whatever it is that has your constant attention is that which you worship.

For the most part during a day, we don't consciously give our attention too much. Everything is quite by rote and memorized muscle movements: eat, shower, dress, work, repeat after sleeping. Since most thought is memorized and perhaps unconscious, it doesn't seem like it would take much time or effort to make your spiritual center be the majority of your conscious thought during a given day.

For instance, if we take one day of our life and consider we sleep for eight hours. Sixteen hours remain. We eat, work, relate, love, and daydream this time away. Do you think that it is reasonable to spend six minutes for every hour you are awake in focused attention to whatever definition of God might be for you, six minutes! It almost seems silly, but if you spend that six minutes every hour you are awake thinking about God, you will be tithing your time in spiritual practice 10 percent. What could life be like with this practice in place?

That may sound daunting to some readers but rest assured if I can do it so can any of you. It starts slowly and purposefully and there is intention behind all of it. Once you have truly started some kind of ritual practice you see that "ritual" is at the heart of spiRITUALity and it is in this place you are ready to dream big dreams.

Your G.I.F.T.S. are the basis for you to take stock in your life. They are your assets and your liabilities. It is important to truly understand the things in your life that can move you forward. It is equally important for you to make friends with those things that could just pull the rug out from underneath you.

CHAPTER 5:

Allowing in Your Dreams

"We do well to listen to this Inner Voice, for it tells us of a life wonderful in its scope; of a love beyond our fondest dreams; of a freedom which the Soul craves."
Ernest Holmes

Dreaming has never been a problem for me. I feel like I grew up in a dream world with a vivid and vibrant imagination. I was the kind of kid who would set up an archeological dig site in my backyard with the expectation of the find of a lifetime. I was an explorer, adventurer, builder of tree houses, and a dreamer.

I remember when I was around eight years old and other boys my age were setting their sights on being firefighters or football players, I announced to my family that I wanted to be President of the United States. What a nightmarish dream that would be, in retrospect. Besides, with my fondness for firefighters and football players, the highest political office in the land might just be out of my reach.

As I got older, I realized that the chasm between dreams and reality was riddled with snares, traps, and worst of all, work. I wasn't afraid of working hard or achieving my dreams, but somewhere along the way I started to question. I questioned everything. Was this or that really what I wanted? Would I be any good at it? Whose dream was it really? I started to question my abilities also. I am not certain where this messaging came from but somewhere it was bellowed into the cavern of my mind, "YOU'RE NOT DOING IT RIGHT!" That same message echoed off the walls of my mind for many years to come, actually until … well, yesterday, and I am on constant guard for it to reverberate yet again.

This is the devastating message that we hear in the past, latch on to, and carry into our present. We all have some messaging like this that we lug around like the ancient mariner's albatross.

If a tree falls in the forest it does in fact make a sound. If I choose not to hear trees fall then I should leave the forest. The same is true with that negative echo chamber of my mind. Just because the sound was made does not mean that I need to listen to it. What life does it bring to my dreams? There is a third answer to the question "Is the glass half full or half empty?" The glass just is the wrong glass.

When I was younger but after my echoing message of impending failure was already bouncing off the walls of my mind, I stopped letting my dreams be generative. I stopped allowing my dreams to dictate the work to be done and instead just went into more of a free flow pattern of living life. Oh sure, I had a general direction but that direction could have easily changed with an overriding current or a well-placed rock. Like a river, I was floating with life or so I thought. I wasn't fighting life or my dreams anymore. I was also smoking a lot of pot.

There is nothing more strip mining to a life full of dreams

Chapter 5

than "a bong-full of really good bud." I thought at the time this was enhancing the experience and I guess in a way it was; just not the experience that I intended. Remember, intention is working whether we are driving the car or floating with the blissful stream of life. It is all on purpose.

I graduated high school and went on to college. Was it always my dream to go to college? Probably not mine, but I wasn't paying for it. Generally, we pay for our own dreams. If I ever have kids, it will be my dream that they all go to college also. So, good job Mom and Dad!

As I write this, I am realizing that I really didn't have many of my own dreams back then. Mom, Dad, and my two sisters all went to college and joined sororities or fraternities and I guess I just did what was expected of me.

I joined a fraternity that was known for being a party house and I decide that I would fit right in there. After one long drug-addled quarter of college, I realized that perhaps it was the fraternity's fault that I was such a delinquent at school. I dropped out of that fraternity, but not before one night on LSD where I had another strange night of dreams. I only remember one of them.

There I am (I think it's me) but everything exists only in that ethereal dreamlike state. I stand perched on the edge of a huge abyss, an uncrossable canyon. My toes curl over the crest of the edge of rock like talons and I am not afraid. More than anything I feel full breasted with life and living.

I take in a full breath and gently step off the edge confidently knowing the next moment. I am in flight. I soar. My wings full of air. Majestically gliding past cliffs and crags yet avoiding all obstacles with ease and grace.

I feel lighter more on one side than the other. My left wing is whole, but scarred along life's flight. My perspective is elevated and panoramic, always new. My sight is clear and returned anew and my message of hope follows me as it wafts off my tail feathers.

Slowly I descend into the protection of the canyon until it opens out to a wide valley. The rocks and crags are fully occupied by all shapes and sizes of my feathered ilk, as though filling an auditorium.

The piercing cacophony of sound would be frightful and deafening to any other beast, but to my ears it is music and the heralding of hope for the future. It is the language of connection, the call of contemplation, and the birdsong of oneness.

I alight on my perch with a million beady eyes focused on me. I open my throat to speak and the cacophony is deafeningly silent. "We are all one," I sing and the birds explode with the song of agreement. And I wake up.

I had this dream several times, not all on drugs, with slightly different details and I have been trying to dissect it ever since that first trip. What a pointless question to ask, "What does the dream mean?" Dreams don't have to be explained or explainable. That's why they get to happen on that much bigger stage of our subconscious. The only connection between dreams and reality may be some neuro-hormonal transmitter long-forgotten by the pineal gland. There doesn't have to be judgment about why this or that. Simple—I was a bird with a bum shoulder that flew in to speak to the masses of other birds about oneness, healing, and the future. NOW, we are getting somewhere.

Chapter 5

For a while now, I have felt like I had a message to share that would help others. I guess that is one reason behind pushing forward with this book. Not because I have the answers for your life, but because I have answers for my own life. Within all of those answers, yours and mine, are the seeds of sameness, oneness, and unity. I know that as I recognize myself in you, you in turn may identify with some piece of yourself in my story. Unless you were a closeted, promiscuous, perverted, meth addict, felon-turned-bow-tie-wearing, openly gay, happily married, Doctor of Nursing, there will be differences in our stories.

There is a line in one of the Twelve Step recovery texts that reads, "Lost dreams awaken and new possibilities arise." It is up to us to awaken our own lost dreams and then to create an environment that nurtures new dreams. The perfect place to create these dreams is after a full understanding of our G.I.F.T.S.

It is not absolutely necessary to inventory your G.I.F.T.S. in order to dream big but I think it will help to focus your dreams into realizable goals.

For instance, I used to dream about being an astronaut or at least being a space traveler. It was a childhood fantasy from watching *Star Trek*, I guess. I am not sure of the current requirements to become an astronaut, but I am pretty sure that with an accurate inventory of my G.I.F.T.S. I will find that being an astronaut may not be the most realistic choice for my life. Besides, if you can count the life in television, I already traveled "where no man has gone before …" when I was an actor in Los Angeles.

"Would you be willing to shave your entire body for this role?" This was the question I was asked in my audition for *Star Trek: The Next Generation*, episode 133 "Unnatural Selection." "Heck, I would shave Gene Roddenberry's entire body for a role on *Star Trek*. Are you kidding?" was not my reply. I only replied with a simple, "Yes, sir."

I am not sure if all the other candidates said "No" to that question and that was why I was left standing by myself in the lobby of some office waiting on the director's deliberation, but I got the role. That one audition led to a week that is still very high up in my most memorable weeks in life. But this is a story about dreams, so let me back up and talk about the talent that was required to land a role on *Star Trek: The Next Generation*.

It started when I made a very conscious decision to drop out of the University of Washington in 1988 and move to Los Angeles to become an actor. After so many years this story almost makes it sound like I made a very intentional decision when in fact, I was spiraling out of control with drugs and alcohol in Seattle and clearly my problem was school, school politics, and Seattle in general. Moving was the most logical choice. I had just lost the election for President of the Associated Students of the University of Washington. The loss may have been related to one of two things; either I was not strong enough in the debates about dealing with Board of Regents or it was because I was addicted to cocaine. Jury is still out on that one (not really).

Clearly, my only option was to take my God-given acting talent and allow the producers and directors in Hollywood

Chapter 5

the opportunity to make me a star. I wonder if that was the cocaine talking or just some deep-seated megalomania. Nevertheless, I packed everything I owned into my Subaru hatchback and drove to L.A.

When I got to the "Welcome to Los Angeles" sign there was no welcoming committee. There was no agent waiting to take me in and make me a star. They were not waiting for me at the Hollywood sign either. I knew I needed to look harder. Maybe I would even take a class in acting or something. Let's just say I had developed a strong belief in the unknown … my screen acting talent. If I could just tap back into some of that belief right now as I write … this book would be a lot easier to write. It amazes me how pervasive my insecurities are and how paralyzing they can be.

I enrolled in a commercial acting class given by Randy Kirby. Most of you have no idea who he is but you have seen his face hundreds of times in commercials, sitcoms, and movies, like *Pink Cadillac*. The class was fun and energizing. I realized somewhere about week five of ten that this life of acting was not going to be easy as pie and I would need to step up my game.

I tried my hand at sleeping with some "directors" and "producers," but it led me nowhere. The gay bars in West Hollywood are full of wannabe "directors" and "producers" making promises with no intention, or ability, to keep. I don't even think they really were directors or producers but I was too naïve to know at the time. I did discover a few true Hollywood movers and shakers, but they were disgustingly not my type.

Fortunately, or unfortunately, I still had enough of my youthful innocence and ideology that I was not yet at the point in life where I would actually prostitute myself to get ahead. It is striking how fine the line is between sleeping with someone you want to sleep with who you think can get you ahead in business and being repulsed by the idea of prostitution. I wasn't repulsed by prostitution in Amsterdam, but perhaps the rules were different when I was out of the country.

The final night of the Randy Kirby class was called "Agents' Night." It was the night we could showcase our talent to a bevy of local talent agents in hopes of getting picked up. It was a potluck and my only culinary claims to fame were Tuna Noodle Surprise and a very creative and spicy Lasagna. The surprise was just parmesan cheese so it was not really all that special. I chose to bring the lasagna.

I thought I performed my commercials adequately both in comedic form and my more serious one. My commercial talent was generally overly comedic to the point of campy or too serious to the point of mass audience wrist slitting. Clearly, I still had work to do. I still had hope that my talent, no matter how raw, would be recognized by one of these entertainment moguls.

We got finished with the entertainment portion of the night and started eating potluck. The agents seemed satisfied or maybe bored and I just wanted them to be satisfied. I desperately wanted an agent.

Toward the end of the evening on Agents' Night, Meryl Jonas of the Irv Schechter Company asked Randy who'd

Chapter 5

made the lasagna. SCORE! She liked me, or at least she liked my lasagna. She asked for the recipe and I told her that I would love to bring it to her office as a way of perhaps sticking my foot in the proverbial door.

Years later, my assessment is that Hollywood is very little about actual talent, not that talent was my strong suit. It really is more about connections and relationships, professional, personal, and intimate, to be in the right place at the right time. For me that day, it was about the relationship of spicy sausage and ricotta cheese. Lasagna, talent or not, I needed an agent and Meryl Jonas was who I selected ... choice of one.

Meryl was super patient with me and she submitted me for as many casting calls as she could. After all, she only makes money if I make money. It's just a numbers game and someone somewhere was bound to give me a shot. There were a few things, like playing Henry Luce in a Time-Warner commercial during the first *Earth Day Special* with Bette Midler playing Mother Earth. The big shot finally came from Junie Lowry Casting, casting agent for *Star Trek*.

The call came in to my pager while I was hanging out with one of my childhood idols, Wesley Eure. I remember watching *Land of the Lost* every Saturday and would echo along with Will, "Run, Holly, run" as they were trying to outlast the dinosaurs. Getting the opportunity to spend time with Wesley in real life was just another childhood fantasy come true. He was generous of spirit and funny to hang out with. I remember laughing intensely with him. One year for Christmas, instead of buying a bunch of presents people may or may not need or like, Wesley made contributions in people's names and let them know with a personal card. I was incredibly touched by the thoughtfulness and mindfulness of this amazing individual.

I had an audition early in the morning in the valley, so I stayed the night closer to the audition in hopes of getting there very early in the morning—10:00 a.m. This was very early living a life where you are in the habit of drinking and partying and doing God-only-knows-what until the wee hours of the morning.

Needless to say, I woke up late, hung over, eyes bloodshot, and probably reeking of everything I'd consumed the night before. I got to the audition thirty minutes late and the lobby was empty. There I stood in a gray tank top, jeans, and a white cardigan sweater with a red stripe like ivy-leaguers wore. A wave of disappointment came over me as I realized that I had missed my one big shot because I was partying too much the night before. I would probably never get another chance at my big break. Always pendulum swinging between never and always, black and white, high and drunk, something had to give. As I was getting ready to walk out and slump back to my car, a door opened.

"Are you here for the audition?"

I explained that I was and that I was sorry for being so late and lied about how bad the traffic was and was ready to add to my already too long story about an eighteen-wheeler blocking two lanes of … when Junie interrupted.

Chapter 5

"Wait right here."

There were several people sitting in the room they led me into, eyeing me like a piece of meat. I am not sure who was in there, but when I tell the story, I say that Gene Roddenberry himself was in the room. It is true in my mind. They had me take off the cardigan sweater and turn around. I felt like I was naked with hot stares burning my tender flesh. The room seemed stuffy and I felt dirty, which was probably just leftover remorse from the night before.

"Would you be willing to shave your body for this role?"

I have never been particularly hairy so I really didn't recognize any gravity in this request but said, "Yes, sir," because it seemed like the thing to say.

"Great, you are hired. We will contact your agency and you will be hearing from us soon."

You know that sound that Scooby Doo makes when he says, "Huh?" That is the sound effect that went through my head. I didn't recite lines or demonstrate any particular talent except to remove my clothes but somehow it was enough. Perhaps it was the way I removed my clothes or at least my sweater. I learned later that they were looking for a particular and very specific type to play a genetically altered, artificially enhanced, perfect twelve-year old boy. I was a tall, dark, handsome twenty-two-year-old, and I guess I fit the type. Right place, right time, well maybe a bit late but I did not have to soil any casting couch, this time.

There is no high quite like getting a role on your all-time favorite show. Things went into warp speed. I had fittings and an appointment to have a full body cast made, hence the body shaving. My wardrobe consisted of short shorts made of long underwear fabric and a full-length, form-fitting Plexiglas body cast like the Visible Man model I had growing up. In one scene, I was fully clothed in a skintight purple jumpsuit but most of the time I was just in the short shorts.

I will never forget that week I spent on the Paramount Studios lot. I had my own trailer with my name on the door. It was written with Sharpie on masking tape but it was my name on my door on my trailer, nevertheless. At least I had a place where I could escape to smoke some pot to relax or to take one of the extras that I was trying to seduce, or both. I was playing up the Hollywood Star role to the hilt.

My fondest memory was just a few seconds long but burned into my memory banks forever. I was pushing out on the stage door to go to my trailer. I was wearing my short shorts with a bathrobe over the top. As I pushed out hard on the door, someone else was pulling back hard on the door and there I was nose-to-nose with the man I wanted my father to be: Captain James Tiberius Kirk. We were so close I could have kissed him without any effort or movement.

"Did we wake you up?" William Shatner said as he took stock of what I was wearing.

"No, sir," was all I could croak out as I stood there in shock.

Star Trek VI was in its final filming and the whole cast from the original series was there on the lot. I had the opportunity to meet them all, thanks to my friend Richard Arnold who was a *Star Trek* continuity expert and consultant for the show. I was invited by Richard to go to the wrap party for this newest movie and was seated next to George Takei who has become one of my favorite Facebook posters.

This time in my life was heaven on earth. It was a dream come true and I was trying to take advantage of every opportunity. Filming the episode was amazing and working with such talented individuals was a highlight of my acting career. Actually, it was my only light in my acting career. It turned out that my talents may have been elsewhere and being a professional actor was not what I was cut out for. I remember telling myself that I would stay in Los Angeles for at least five years to make a go of this new career and I made it three years before I moved back to Seattle in 1990 to finish my Political Science degree.

Los Angeles was a good diversion for me and I would not be the person I am today had it not been for all of the experiences that I had there. I dreamed I could make it. I put the plan in motion. There just were certain threats to progress that got in the way there. L.A. was where I first recognized that I had a problem with addiction and it was where I sought help for the first time. That is when Wesley Eure saved my life.

I was drinking, heavily, every night. Generally, I would drink in West Hollywood at the Mother Lode or Revolver or some seedier gay bar that fed my hunger. I always had about a thirty-minute drive home and I always drove home drunk whether it was my home or someone else's home. I even woke up one Sunday morning on a blanket in an abandoned field right off the Sunset Strip with some random guy. Thank God there were condom wrappers amongst the debris field that surrounded our blanket.

I was on a collision course with life when I met Wesley. He was kind and full of love and very patient with me. Most people had to be by the time I had reached this stage. I was spinning out of control. He introduced me to his friends and we genuinely had a good time together no matter what we were doing. The only time we stopped having a good time is when I crossed over that imaginary line of having had enough to drink and too much. The final night was a quiet dinner at El Coyote with him and his friend Susan Lucci. I found her interesting, but Wesley was giving her way more attention than he was giving me and I got more and more annoyed as I drank. Finally, I stood up, pushed back my chair from the table, and announced dramatically that I was going home and he could call me later. I stormed out. In my mind, I am sure I didn't even say goodnight to Susan but that may be a scene I am replaying from one of her soap opera episodes in my mind and not the actual truth.

He did call me that night. I don't remember everything we talked about but I know he had a very kind tone. He always did. He started explaining a story to me about a conversation he was having with his psychic in New York. The psychic told him he was spending a lot of time with someone who was an alcoholic and he thought it was me.

Chapter 5

Rather than focusing on the direct problem, I deflected. "Are you spending a lot of time with someone else?" I questioned accusingly. When he said, "No," my fate was sealed.

He asked if I would go to a recovery meeting with his friend Scott the next day and that was the first time I admitted I had a problem. I was an alcoholic. January 6, 1989 was not the last time I used any substances because I still had more story to write, but it was the first time I surrendered to the possibility of a better life and I have Wesley to thank for that, or at the very least his psychic in New York.

It is easy to say that I am living my dreams, but is that really true? Was it my dream to go to college or was it someone else's dream for my life that was handed down through constant and continuous reinforcement. Many things in our formative years that mistakenly are described as "our dreams" are merely someone else's dreams for us. I want to be clear; this does not make them bad or wrong, just not authentically ours.

Dreaming is important and although I began this chapter with a written description of a dream during sleep, I believe "awake" dreams are where the true generation of intention resides. There is no means in man's existence more powerful for setting one's intention than the simple daydream. What actually is a dream?

There are many definitions of dreams. Many would more suitably be called nightmares; like the dream of being the President or an astronaut for that matter. A dream in context with living an intentional life is very simply the highest form of expression a life can conceive in the areas of health, wealth, love, and creative expression.

These can be born out of the subconscious sleep-state dreams of phantasmagorical proportions but will only truly take hold when we bring them up into consciousness. Then maybe we are more aptly referring to "day dreams" as they take hold in the light of day (or night for my Night Shift nursing friends who "day" dream).

It really doesn't matter if they are called hopes, wishes, wants, desires, or dreams; they are the DNA that maps out a life lived with intention. The DNA is then coiled purposefully in on itself until it fits perfectly into the seed of thought.

Take my dream to be a published author, for instance. This is not a new desire. I am not exactly sure where it came from or how old it is for me. Perhaps it was on the coattails of wanting to be President and then writing my own memoirs as I sit sipping champagne at an antique desk overlooking Cape Cod. I always wanted a life that was exciting enough to write about. Aha! There is the DNA of that dream. "Be careful what you wish for," I have heard it said and this is proof. I did get my wish and it absolutely did NOT look as I had planned it out in my mind.

The first conscious recollection of moving toward wanting to be an author that I can remember was many years ago. I kept a journal of daily life and thoughts. It actually was the most consistent thing that I did on an almost daily basis except for using meth. The journals became the diary of a meth addict really. I remember thinking that someday these writings would be published. Reading them today, I find them confusing, enlightening, and sad all at once.

I wrote bold treatises and discourses on Freedom and Justice that trail off into indecipherable drivel as I fell asleep at the pen. There are poems in these journals that have deep, rich, disturbed layers of thought only to end mid-sentence without so much as an ellipsis.

It was actually one of these poems, however, that first got my attention to publish. The poem is entitled "The Outcast Lunch Bunch" and it is a wonderful story of friendship between animals born with stark differences that they overlook and get along anyway. These animals are drawn together to form a world full of love and acceptance.

I wrote this poem on a lunch break from a temp job working at some tech support job in downtown Seattle. I took my lunch to a place called Waterfall Park in Pioneer Square and looked up at the rocks and just started writing. It was inspired writing that I did not have to think about at all. It just flowed out of the pen onto the page. I was not actively high when I wrote it; however, with the time it takes for drugs to be washed out of the body I was always "on drugs" at that time in my life. The poem was written in forty-five minutes and only had six crossed out words on the page. I can't really take the credit for the content but I did write it down, listening to that inner voice.

The Outcast Lunch Bunch

High up from the valley below sat Misha and Deery,
a mouse and a doe.
An odd pair made the duo, a sight to see twice.
For deer never hang out with rabbits or mice.

"It's queer" said the owl, from whence wise-marks told.
"To see such a sight in our subtundra fold."

But Misha the mouse and Deery, doe deer were friends
with each other
In spite of the fear.
The fear that somehow they would not behold.
The others they knew in that subtundra fold.

But the friends held steadfast in light of cold stares.
As a matter of fact they befriended the bears.
Bo bear and Baby bear, Mamooshka and Stan.
Imagine the cold stares, you probably can.

The other mammals, aves and fauna
Hatefully looked on as Robin and Llona
Joined up with the strangest collection of creatures,
A turtle and a mule with similar features.

Both Robin the turtle and Llona the mule
Wore frowns of the lonely, the sad and the cruel.

"Why frown?" asked Misha, the mouse next to Deery
"Frowning is sad and you both should be cheery."

"Cheery and why?" asked the mule with a burr.
"They don't understand us, they hate us for sure.

Chapter 5

We are outcasts like you mouse, Deery and bears,
The turtle and I and a few slow arriving hares."

"Yes" piped the mouse
"We are outcasts and it is great,
We are no longer part of the corruption and hate
We love one another without care or fuss
No matter the phylum, species or genus

"The race and the creed matter no more
Religion is love and no basis for war
It is a world where we outcasts can live with each other
Bound together by love, my sisters and brothers."

I remember slamming the journal shut right after the ink dried on the last word and a giddiness came over me like I was goosed by the hand of God. "That's good," I squealed out loud to no one in particular, yet to everyone.

I read that poem to so many people over the next few months that I committed it to memory, even to this day. I recited it to this one gentleman whom I respected at the time. I am not really sure why I respected him, but I remember that I called him "Coach" and don't know why I did that either. Coach and I were driving around Seattle and he was giving me fatherly advice that I was readily accepting along with expensive G.I.F.T.S. and dinners. It's actually more of a common gay-coming-out story than one might think. I was telling him about my poem and that I dreamed of being a published author some day. I had yet to read the poem to Coach. I thought there might have even been a chance that he would have thought it was a dumb children's poem with words that are too big for children to understand.

He finally convinced me to share it with him as we were parked in his big fancy car in Volunteer Park. He listened quietly, gently laughing at the built-in illustrative ridiculousness. When I finished I noticed he was tearing up. He hugged me and told me that he thought it was good, really good. I remember his words, "That, my boy, is the next "twas the night before Christmas.'" I wasn't sure exactly what he meant by that but it was like fuel to the fire of my dreams.

I don't know what became of Coach. I may have gotten too old for him or perhaps he was looking for some commitment and consistency. Neither of these were attributes that I had acquired during this time in my life. I was still on my downward spiral after all, even if I had bright moments like this poem.

In prison, I met this guy who claimed to be a great children's book illustrator. His drawings were all right and I would need an illustrator if I were ever to publish this book. What do they say about necessity being the father of invention? I needed cute woodland creatures and this guy could draw cute woodland creatures. The fact that we were both locked up in prison was merely an inconvenience.

We became friends and spent our limited time together walking around the track in "The Yard" and talking about what illustrations I needed him to do for the book. I remember putting energy into mapping out the storyboard and making sure that the drawings each spoke to the

Chapter 5

stanza that would be on it. At the time, it felt like a regular partnership, like Rodgers and Hammerstein, Gershwin and Gershwin, or Streisand and Bacharach except those pairs had something we did not have … Freedom.

Looking back on this project from today's vantage point, I am surprised I never got the book published. Today, though, I know why I didn't. I hadn't done the steps to move the dream into reality. I had not taken stock in my life, inventoried my G.I.F.T.S. Heck, at that time in my life I was more riddled by I. and T. than anything else. Insecurities and Threats to progress were my daily fare. I guess freedom would have fallen into the Threats to progress category.

I still haven't published that book, although I still talk about it from time to time. I did, however, finally realize my dream of becoming a published author. I submitted one of my other shorter poems to a contest for an anthology of poems called "Nature's Echoes." The poem was a goofy poem called "Poor Petunia" that I wrote in some drug-addled state.

Poor Petunia

Poor Petunia, wind-blown, she was
Hair all strewn with sticks and fuzz.
She sat, as her skirt took on air
And the fuzz and sticks flew out of her hair.

Saddened by the loss of the fuzz and sticks
Petunia jumped up, tall, on the bricks.
Prepared not for such and away she flew
And went she did to where the wind blew.

Was I Petunia? Blowing with the wind? This really doesn't give much permanence or foundation for a life of dreams fulfilled. I knew life needed to change. Not in the same way I knew I needed to renew my driver's license, but this knowing was on a much deeper, less identifiable level. I guess this is where I started to dream of life being different, better, brighter, more on purpose.

Our dreams can be the very seed of hope we need to change life itself. To dream into the seed all of the positive things imagined but yet to be. Then the seed is packed away in stasis just waiting for the right time and environment for germination.

I dreamed from a very early age of helping people. Dreams are like the general "what" for your life and the "how" ends up being like a game show with unlimited doors to try and see if that gets you to your "what." In wanting to help people, I did not dream of being a drug dealer or prostitute, but on some level, I was helping people there too. It was not until that moment when I had the clarity of being a nurse that life began to move in the direction of my dreams. I had found what's behind Door Number 3. Now my dreams could start being crafted into my life's goals.

CHAPTER 6:

Crafting Your Goals

"A goal is a dream with a deadline."
Napoleon Hill

A dream that is dreamt enough in waking hours becomes a goal. Do I have goals? Yes, of course I do. Did I have goals when I was steeped in my drug addiction? Again, of course I did. However, there is not some magical ascension to success simply because you have a dream or this would have been a six-step process. There is actually more work to do. Dreaming is a start but then you need to expand your life out into the world.

I remember when my life had become so small that no matter how hard I tried I could not make it beyond a five-mile radius from my house, if I could make it out of my house at all. That doesn't mean I did not have a goal to go further than the Seattle city limits. I remember when I was truly enmeshed in the disease of addiction I would dream of going to Italy, New York, or even the beach on the Washington Coast. One might even say I talked about these things so much they were actual goals. That being true, even going to the store to buy groceries was a goal, but more often than not getting high took precedence. The drugs held me chained to myself, unable to commit to an over-dreamt dream.

The funny thing about goals is they can be like driving a

car, riding a bus, or white-water rafting. When you are in the driver's seat, you decide where you want to go. When you're on a bus, you are on someone else's schedule, relying on other people to set your goals. For the adrenaline junkie, there is the chaotic life of free white water ready to go plummeting over a cliff at every turn. This sounds like it could be fun in the right circumstances and with the right safety equipment, but there I go being all pragmatic and responsible. My story did not always end up so safely to say the least, but there were smooth patches.

I remember happily floating down the river that was my sophomore year of high school. I was fifteen. That seems to be the chasm between not knowing anything and knowing you don't know anything. A bridge once crossed never to be crossed again. "Ignorance is bliss," they say. Once you know that, however, it is too late. But there I was, blissfully happy. I think I was Sophomore Class President, but don't fully remember. The critical thing was that I had caught the eye of some in the administration at my High School as having POTENTIAL.

God, I loathe that word: potential. Growing up I received report cards stating I was a social butterfly, but these graduated to "George would do better in school if he would perform up to his potential." The dreadful classes I sat through to receive such enlightening critiques would have been vastly more scintillating had my teachers also performed to their potential. But, ah, there we are, creatures of potential waiting to be actualized and activated.

One day I was called into the school counselor's office for

a meeting. I am not sure that I even knew at the time that we had a school counselor because, as previously stated, I was blissfully happy. Now, that bridge had been crossed. We sat down and she explained to me that I had been selected to represent our high school at the Hugh O'Brian Youth Leadership Weekend. The whole thing sounded great to me. It's like white-water rafting; it always starts out calm and by the time you realize just how real it is, it is too late.

Many of you might remember Hugh O'Brian as Wyatt Earp. I remember his rugged, no-nonsense frontier lawman swagger. He also started a foundation that helps nurture and encourage future world leaders. I was going to what? How cool was that!

Sophomores from all over the country gathered first in their home state to compete like some kind of leadership hunger games. Then we would send one boy and one girl from each state conference to the national weekend. Instead of trying to kill each other, like in the movies, we were put in groups to discuss core values like volunteerism, integrity, excellence, diversity, and community partnership. Wyatt offered sophomores a vehicle to realize their goals and determine their own future. For a kid like me who had decided he wanted to be President of the United States at the age of eight, this was a dream weekend. Except that I would have to perform up to my potential! Later in life if I had attended a conference like this I would have just asked, "Where is the bar?"

I wish, sometimes, that I could have talked about how driven I was to realize my goals. I wish I could say that from a three-day leadership camp I was catapulted into the driver's seat of my intentional life. I would claim that I methodically steered course to the finish line of my goals, but that was not my story or my path. I was not able to take the steering wheel on my life until much later. I did get on the bus though. This bus was safe and comfortable and, in retrospect, I found out it made two important stops for my life: performance and friendship.

There were hundreds of kids at this weekend camp, but I only remember two: Shari and Barrie. Each of these girls had a special bus stop for my life, although neither stop was putting me in the White House. After all, it was white water not the White House that was pulling me.

The friendships forged at camp were nurtured over the years in high school and college. I stayed friends with both Shari and Barrie throughout that time. I was even their date to this or that event in our respective houses in the Greek System. Sororities are full of girls looking for the "safe" date and I certainly fit that bill. The ironic part is that each of their mothers really wanted their relationship with me to be more than a friendship.

Looking back on it, who could blame them? I was a kind, polite young man with good manners from a good family that they had met at youth leadership camp. I was every parent's dream for their daughters except for a few small details. The biggest of which is that I was and have always been gay, but there were a few other smaller issues. For one of the girls I was too much a bad boy, drinking with my fraternity brothers. For the other or her mother at least, I

Chapter 6

wasn't Jewish. The important roles that each of these women played in my life became apparent after I moved back to Seattle from Los Angeles in 1990.

When I moved back from Los Angeles, I realized that I had been infected with some kind of performance bug. I always had a love for performing and found opportunities to play a character or a role, even if it was in real life. It was as if my life had become a play and I was "acting" like a student, an employee, or a friend.

It was one of these moments when I was "acting" like a student in a local coffee shop, that my goal to perform took another leap. I actually was a student finishing my senior year in Political Science, but life was sometimes difficult to discern from art and it was all rather surreal. One thing that I know for sure is that I was sober at the time because I stayed that way until very soon after I graduated.

In that coffee shop, I saw a sweet familiar face from my past. Shari was there and she remembered me. She remembered not that I was some leader from the Hugh O'Brian leadership weekend, but that I was a performer and she was looking for performers right now! Actually, it was her mother, Lynda who was on the hunt for performers.

Lynda was the producer of a benefit show at Seattle's 5th Avenue Theater called "Follies at the 5th." She needed another male in the category of tall, dark, and handsome. Lynda and I had met at least one time in the past, perhaps more. I am not certain. What I am certain of the day I met Lynda is that I was instantly drawn to this woman.

If my goal was to be a star then Lynda was sent from

heaven to make it so. She saw potential, that word again, in me that I never saw in myself. When she looked at me, she saw a vaudevillian performer, a tap dancer, a singer, a star. She made me feel so incredibly high on ego-boosting endorphins that I don't know why I ever left her side.

I showed up for rehearsal a few weeks before we went on stage with Follies and in those few weeks I was thrust up front in seven different numbers and I was on top of the world. I was performing!

The transitions and timeline of my life get very fuzzy after this time. I know that I performed many times with Lynda as a singer and a dancer. One day she called me to pitch an idea. She wanted me to be George M. Snickerdoodles, Esq. She said that I was sure to be the next J.P. Patches (a local television show favorite in Seattle) and children everywhere would know me and adore me. I was hooked by this bug, but unfortunately I was hooked by another bug too that turned out to be stronger.

My goal to finish college had been realized, but there was nothing to follow it up. There had been no class in senior year to set new goals. No one had said, "This will be your next step." My work with Lynda and Snickerdoodles was fun but it was not consistent enough and did not pay the bills. I loathed the idea of being a "starving artist" and I needed new goals. I found methamphetamines instead.

Meth is like the nuclear solution for dreams, goals, and life in general. Anything going well will be gone and anything in the crapper will be flushed and any steamy piles will only get worse. My life was becoming a steamy pile … warm and comfortable from my perspective.

Chapter 6

At this time, I was living up in Index, Washington at the gay campground for the summer. There were semi-permanent campsites set up in lavish style befitting a solely gay clientele. There was also every permutation of addiction that one could think of there on the shores of the North Fork of the Skykomish River.

Being a performer was a goal realized, but that summer there were some very ironic twists that were not quite what I expected. It was the Fourth of July in the early 1990s, a year when Seattle was living up to its reputation of having summer start on the Fifth of July. Most of the day I was miserable and the rest of the day was a blur.

Lynda had secured a stage for Snickerdoodles and Company to perform at the Fourth of July Celebration at the park on Elliott Bay. The thing about a fast-moving show that includes frequent costume changes and tons of frenetic energy is that it is a perfect disguise for a budding meth addict. The problem with so many costume changes is that I have to wear at least three costumes at once, one on top of the other. With the heat of the costume itself and the meth-induced internal fire I was usually sweating like a whore in church. Not what you want from a children's performer.

The weather that day was unpredictable and really downright schizophrenic. Just before the show was to start, the heavens opened up and it rained harder than I ever remember it raining in Seattle. Big soaking drops that fall out of sky and sink into your bones even if you have three costumes on, one on top of the other. I was so wet you could see costume number three through costume number one. The show went on in a soggy, sweaty, frenetic slog complete with damp puppets. Looking back, it was like a bad trip down Sesame Street.

Maybe the rain was sent to purify my soul for what would be the rest of my performing that night. I was hired for another show that night. One that was definitely not for kids. As I drove the long road from downtown Seattle and ascended into the mountains, I realized that my standards and morals were descending to new depths. That morning I was a paid children's performer and that night I was a paid erotic stripper in a gay campground. The irony of my life hit me as I passed through Monroe and started up into the mountains. I had to pull my car to the side of the road and spent a few moments in tears and laughter mixed in the cauldron of irony. I was back to the duality that had defined my life but I thought that I was realizing my goals of wanting to perform. Perhaps it was quality of experience I was looking for, not quantity.

Goals are measurable. They are attainable. They are like a big to-do list in life. Become a performer, check. Get addicted to drugs, check. Try your hand at stripping, prostitution, and porn, check, check, and … still a yet (gotcha). Go to prison, get off drugs, and become a doctor, check, check, and check. But what about the goals that seem to be intangible and unmeasurable like becoming a good person and maintaining friendships. For goals such as this you need a good yardstick or barometer, something with which to compare yourself. Thanks to Hugh O'Brian, I had just the thing with Barrie.

Chapter 6

From the start, I observed how Barrie cultivated and nurtured friendships like a master gardener tends to an arboretum. It was clear that she was different and special right from the start. There was an affable quality to her at fifteen that was infectious and people were drawn to her energy.

This sort of quality does not change much as we get older. It only gets better and richer. I would say it ages like a fine wine but that seems entirely inappropriate in a book with addiction as the antagonist. Barrie has always demonstrated to the world a method of being a friend. I don't know if she could even put to words what she does to nurture her friendships. She just does. In a way, she helped me craft my goal to be a good and nurturing friend way back then.

She describes me now as the perfect date back then, handsome but not "handsy" with a sense for fashion, a flare for drama, and a desire to shop. I have lost some sense, flare, and desire as I have aged—but still. Her mother still wants us to get married even though I am still not Jewish and Barrie has repeatedly told her that my husband would not approve.

Barrie is in my life today in my closest of circles. It was not always the case. Sometimes in the realizing of your goals, you get off the path. Sometimes it is the only way to truly know where the path is. My time foraging for life under rocks and dirt taught me what friendship does not look like. I learned what it felt like to not be in my definition a "good" person. At least, it did not feel good when I was in it.

Drugs, Food, Sex and *God*

I will never forget the day that Barrie and I returned to each other's lives. It was like a slow motion running beach hug except without the romantic music and we were in the middle of Barnes & Noble in front of the blank journals. It was the right place at the right time. I was ready to find my way again to my goal of being a good person and maintaining friendships and now my teacher was back in my life.

Barrie is one of my best friends and closest confidantes. She was one of the first people I told that I wanted to marry Travis and was one of three on my side in the wedding party. By the way, I selected the most hideous blue taffeta monstrosity for her to wear in the wedding party, to which she very politely just said, "Uh, no."

Why did I become a Doctor Nurse? This is a reasonable question for which I have many answers. The funniest and maybe the most accurate is so Carol Baxter could tell everyone about her son, the doctor. But the story started when another doctor in my life planted a seed that helped craft this goal.

I had just been laid off my job as a marketing specialist for a company that made Linux servers. I barely know what Linux is, so being the marketing guy was clearly not the job for me. It was not, shall we say, in my wheelhouse. Before I was the marketing guy, I was one of the programming guys ... it was actually amazing that the dumb things worked. Marketing was something I had demonstrated that I could handle after all; I went to prison around sales and marketing, technically. Clearly laying me off was just a nice way of putting me out of my misery.

Chapter 6

I was getting all of my doctor and dentist appointments out of the way to get "tuned up" before going on unemployment, a benefit I did not have in my previous sales job.

My doctor asked me what I would do next and I shrugged my shoulders in a way of saying "Don't know, don't care." But I did care, I was so scared. I had come such a long way to putting my life back together. I had just passed the one-year mark in my recovery from drugs and I was living on my own (with roommates) and paying my bills for the first time in a long time. I felt like I had the world by the balls, if the world had balls, and then this happened. I was terrified for my life.

"You are a smart guy; why not go into medicine?" said my doctor with more confidence about my abilities than I certainly had.

I met this doctor while he was still in residency. He was the one who took care of me when I was so full of staph infection at University Hospital. He watched from the sidelines as I spun my life out of control and downward on meth and alcohol, and stuck with me while I was in prison. He had seen my transformation after getting clean and was amazed by the phoenix rising from the ashes of my burned-out life. He wanted me to fly and not the way I had in the past but really have my life soar.

"I am too old to become a doctor, now, Doc," I declared with my newly found defeatist attitude. I was thirty-seven.

"Well, there are other things to do in medicine than to be a doctor," was his only reply.

As I walked out and said goodbye to my friend Carole,

his nurse, and the medical assistants and front office staff who had all become my friends I realized that all of these people were "in medicine." The seed was firmly planted and I began to nurture this newly crafted goal.

A close friend was working on her prerequisites to become a nurse. She had mentioned nursing school to me on more than one occasion, but I had dismissed it as just a great idea for her. This was before my job situation had changed. All at once, I was interested in what she was doing and where she was going to school because it now served my interest. Drug addiction makes a person profoundly self-centered and the recovery from self-absorption is slow.

A nurse … huh … I wonder if I could be a nurse. I had never given a speck of thought to this idea before that moment in the doctor's office. Whether I had thought of it before or not there is a feeling that comes over you when the Universe presents you with the truth of your life. The feeling is indisputable and undeniable. There is no argument and nowhere to run. It is principle and principle has no opposite. That was the feeling that welled up from deep in my soul that day and is with me to this moment.

I became a nurse and realized that it was a goal that suited me well. The entire time I was in school, I felt that this nursing career was just a start, just a doorway into a bigger and brighter future.

It is wonderfully organic how one goal in life leads to another. There is so much of being a nurse where having the confidence of being a performer is key. Shari and Lynda helped me to develop these essential skills. Friendship and

Chapter 6

kindness, modeled by Barrie, have become a major part of the very fiber of who I am. Who I am is a nurse, first. While becoming a nurse I was called to greater service watching a well-dressed nurse in a long white coat expertly care for some cardiac patients and their families, and I knew my next step was to become like her, a nurse practitioner. As a nurse practitioner, my patients frequently called me "Doctor" presumably because I was a man in a white coat with a stethoscope. I guess being a Doctor Nurse was just the next step. One small goal led to the next but it was in that conversation with Doctor Matt that the seed was planted. He said "medicine," I heard "doctor," the Universe heard me hear "doctor," I became a nurse, and the rest just fell into place. I became Doctor Nurse George.

CHAPTER 7:

SETTING THE PLAN

"Life happens when you are making other plans."
Lyrics of "Beautiful Boy" by John Lennon

Although John Lennon used the above line in a lyric in the song "Beautiful Boy," it was really Allen Saunders who had the earliest notation for having coined the phrase. Funny thing is that Saunders probably used the line in his *Mary Worth* comic strip. Remember *Mary Worth*? Selling her apples on the street and dishing out wisdom and advice with her red deliciousness. There were so many *Mary Worth* stories about drugs and alcohol, if only I had listened to Mary. Looking back on it now, I thought Mary was an old busybody and needed to leave those kids alone. I wonder how many people I speak with feel the same way.

I have news for Ms. Worth and Mr. Saunders: Life happens because of your plans not in spite of them. There is purposefulness in life. I frequently say that my life is a straight line when I look at it in retrospect. However, I believe that if it has a purpose and a pattern looking back on it then it has a pattern looking to the future as well.

Plans are those lists of specific things to do, get, say, or accomplish in order to move on toward your celebration of having accomplished your intention. Plans should not be confused with the actual "doingness" of things.

Plans are more cerebral, less hands-on than action. Plans

Drugs, Food, Sex and *God*

look more like drawings, to-do lists, and class syllabi than anything else. Although action can be taken without specific plans, I contend that it is a plan in and of itself and is the "no-plan" plan and potentially a very dangerous plan indeed.

I went into prison weighing in at a wet 185 pounds and I came out eight months later at 228 pounds and proceeded up to 242 pounds by the time I was done building my protective coating. They say when you put down the spoon you pick up the fork. This is not a reference to proper utensil etiquette from Miss Manners, but rather a very dark reference to the exercise involved with intravenous drug use and the use of the bent spoon as a "sauce pan," if you will. Truth be told the nasty poison I injected didn't need to be cooked again; it would dissolve in just about anything including Orange Crush on the back of a pop can. I always wondered if that fed my carbohydrate cravings.

I have always appreciated what Marianne Williamson says about excess weight. She talks about visualizing the weight as a brick wall that you build and carry around with you to separate yourself from other people and from life itself. It is like building a castle wall for protection; at least it was the case for me. I never realized at the time, but I was unconsciously, yet methodically, building my own walls in prison. I didn't have some plan for obesity, but like many plans, they are drawn up in the dark recesses of our mind without conscious thought.

Building my castle wall started when I first arrived at Washington Corrections Center in Shelton, Washington

Chapter 7

in the fall of 1999. I was thirty-three. A string of us all chained together were slowly led off the transport bus and into the Intake Center. It was like a chain gang from some old prison movie, exactly like it. Each of us was scared and showing it in our own particular brand of psychopathology. I was being funny and cute, not a big seller in prison. I was completely out of place like some big cosmic joke. I felt like a giraffe in a field full of cows, not an uncommon feeling in my life. This time was different though; my usual coping mechanisms were not working at all. I wasn't able to be a chameleon and just fit in with these men.

It seemed that the most prevalent image was that of a "tough guy," so I tried that one on for a second until I got beat up for calling someone a "punk." Who knew that "punk" was such an unpopular word in an institution full of lonely desperate men. I certainly did not mean it the way it was taken.

I was so scared. I was so completely out of my comfort zone and I can only imagine the look that I perpetually had on my face. There was a group of guys that seemed to sniff out fear and capitalize on it. "Fag," they would spit at me as they passed me in the hall or outside in the "yard." I thought it would pass. I thought they would stop, but they just kept it up. I tried to keep my head down and my mouth shut in hopes that they would find some other target, but enough was enough. The second I lifted my head to talk back, I was elbowed in the stomach and punched in the head.

"Fags don't talk, they just suck dick," the jerk in charge

declared. I went back to my cell to try and hide or turn invisible. I cried.

Let's just say, I was too tall to hide, too skinny to fight, too smart for my own good, too stupid to know better, and totally and completely defenseless in this new world. So I ate.

I remember getting uniforms at one point early on and quickly went from an XL orange jumpsuit to an XXL. I was oddly comforted by the extra roominess of my new orange bubble. My cellmate was working in the laundry and I remember asking him to bring me an XXXL jumpsuit back just to see how much better it would feel to have the space.

The food in prison is meant to keep the natives from being restless and it was anything but gourmet. To call it carb-heavy is to say Mount Everest makes for a nice hike. It was a steady diet of potatoes, bread, rice, more potatoes, and scraps of meat. I easily filled up my castle wall just like I planned. I just never realized that I had planned it until later thanks to Marianne Williamson.

When I was released from prison, I had clothes sent in for me to wear home. The shame and embarrassment I felt at not being able to button or zip up my pants was overwhelming. I was free from behind the prison walls only to be trapped in this new "protective" castle.

I wanted to lose the weight but I had no plan. I even made an effort to return to my original weight-loss plan, methamphetamines, but that only resulted in a visit to my probation officer and me needing to explain how my weight-loss plan had gone amiss.

A plan is well thought-out and sometimes best if written.

Chapter 7

We have all seen plans. Imagine purchasing a bookcase from IKEA and not following the plan that is provided to put it together. I don't know about you, but the times that I thought the task was easy enough, that I didn't need a plan, I ended up with three very substantial looking extra pieces and a wobbly bookcase.

My probation officer had a plan for me. Even had it written down. He showed me my urinalysis when it came back positive for methamphetamines, a fact about which I incredulously tried to feign my innocence. Nice try. Scott, my very patient Community Corrections Officer, informed me that I was welcome to choose to go back to prison to serve the rest of my time (Plan A) or get serious about getting my life on track (Plan B). He had a plan. Either choice was fine with him and choice "A" was even preferable because after the initial paperwork it would make his job easier to have me back in prison.

It was at this fork in the road that I had another spiritual awakening. I could not imagine myself spending one more day in the tattoo playland for thugs and punks, so I chose Plan B, whatever that was.

Turns out, Plan B was a life sentence that I am still serving thanks to Scott. From that day, my life changed for the better. The plan included getting active in a recovery program and getting a sponsor. I did each of these things with the gratitude of a free man; after all, the other option was to be just another punk in prison. I still shudder at the thought.

From then on, my life became focused on a program of

action. For every individual action in life, it helps to have a plan even if it is just a loose one. I found that planning was the only way that I could chart my course and recognize my progress toward its completion. It is like knowing you are on step four of six on the freaking bookcase and praying that this time you won't have significant extra pieces. They always included some minor extra screws and dowels but nothing that looks load-bearing.

Speaking of bearing a load, I had to do something about my weight. I was uncomfortable in my body. I no longer recognized my silhouette. I remember one time we were putting on a talent show and I was asked to be the Master of Ceremonies for the show. I decided that because of my extra girth I could play a role I dreamed of playing as a small boy, Alfred Hitchcock.

Mr. Hitchcock was well known for hiding behind a curtain in silhouette and stepping into a cartoon outline of a fat man. Well, I did that for the opening of the talent show. It got a great laugh and was a big success but really only funny in a very sad, sad way. Something needed to change. I needed a plan. It was not for another ten years' suffering from obesity that I was finally able to realize that plan.

It always helps to be organized enough to write your plan down but sometimes life comes at us too quickly. What is important, whether you write your plan down or not, is that you let go of attachment to an outcome. Release the need and desire to control the outcome of your plan and amazing things happen. Pain is what comes from resistance and friction. When it comes to Spirit, or the Borg, resistance is futile. Allow Spirit into the plan and allow divine patterns to present themselves.

I remember years later talking with one of my "sponsees" about his plans. He was getting caught up in having to do this and having to do that and was getting quite anxious in the "having to." He was telling me a story about riding the bus back from an appointment and worrying about whether he was going to find a job and a place to live. He was starting to feel his palms sweat sitting on the bus because of his anxiety and looked out the bus window. He looked up just in time to see some well-placed graffiti; "Everything is Fine," it said. He knew immediately that his plans were on the right track. I laughed when he told me this story because I used to pray to God to give me a sign and not be subtle about it.

My first job out of my Master of Nursing program was the cardiology clinic that I briefly mentioned in the introduction of this book. The fact that it has gotten this much mention is truly amazing because it was the worst job I have ever had and I have had a bunch of them. I would rather just forget about it, but it led me to making my next plan.

I was so disgusted by the level of disrespect levied by the physicians in that practice toward myself and everyone working "underneath" them that I arrived at work every day with the urge to throw up in the parking lot. I wanted to leave that job every single day of the last year I worked there.

It is amazing how a level of unhappiness can manifest

itself in the abandonment of self-care. Have you ever found yourself unhappy or discontent because of how you thought you were being treated and then started mistreating yourself with self-harming behaviors? Does this make any sense? I didn't have my usual vices to turn to, you know, smoking, drinking, or social meth use. I was left back with my old friend food for comfort. What I know today is that any of these behaviors can be done in a way that is obsessive or compulsive and leads to harm. I even tried getting hooked on working out and only managed consistently to exercise my ability to pay my membership fee but was absent from working out for far too long. Every day I would drive by Gold's Gym with the intention of getting back there and restarting my workout. It was a goal without a plan.

Finally, I had enough of the dysfunctional clinic and made a call to the recruiter at the Medical Center connected with the clinic. I told him that he needed to find me some other place to work or I was going to join a circus or do something equally crazy. My plan was to go on vacation from work and give my notice upon my return. If I had another job, great, if not, well then so be it. I surrendered. I believe it was in that surrender that Spirit opened the doors to my future and gently led me through. Had there been a sign it would have read, "Everything is Fine."

I got a call from the recruiter a few days before my vacation. He asked if I could interview at the Bariatric Clinic the Thursday before I left. Bariatrics is the study and treatment of weight-related problems like obesity. Weight Loss

Chapter 7

Services ... I wondered if someone was trying to tell me something. I did not have the level of faith that I have today but looking back on this situation, I see the perfection in the divine plan, better than I could have written.

I was leaving for two weeks on Friday so Thursday was cutting it close but doable. I never imagined working with this patient population but what I know today is I would not be writing this book if it had not been for that job interview. I immediately felt like I had found a place where I could thrive and flourish. I had no idea that the added benefit of getting my weight under control and my health back would be there for me as well. It was like continuing to smoke while working in cardiology. No one is going to listen to an obese weight-loss provider, was my thought. Following the program was my plan.

I followed the plan that I have now used for literally thousands of patients. Following the plan worked! Not that I should be surprised. I didn't have to struggle anymore. I didn't have to follow something that was challenging or expensive. The plan was easy and the actions were celebrated by my success each week losing one to three pounds. I was thriving personally and professionally. I was following the same plan as my patients and because of that we were able to talk together about our progress. I was able to say, "Well, when I was faced with that, this is what I did." It wasn't just some doctor telling them what to do. I was actually doing it and I wasn't a doctor, at least not just yet.

I guess ever since the first suggestion that I should go into medicine I have thought about being a doctor. I just did not want to follow the medical model. While I was at the University of Washington, they were just starting a program called Doctor of Nursing Practice (DNP). It was a relatively new idea and universities were starting to institute programs to meet this new demand. The goal of the DNP program was to prepare clinical nurses for leadership, business, and education, to transform and translate nursing knowledge to a higher level. That is where the dream and the goal started, but the plan seemed daunting. How would I survive two more years of school in a doctoral program and still be able to eat, because I obviously loved doing that?

Making plans takes patience and perseverance. I remember one day at the cardiology clinic staring out the window like Rapunzel waiting for some savior to rescue me from my imprisonment; the victimhood is woefully overstated. I found myself led to Google. Isn't it amazing how powerful the Universal Spirit is? Knowing that we would evolve as human beings into more of human doings with Attention Deficit Disorder, Spirit imbued the power of Creating the Internet to a mystic called Al Gore and the Internet was born. No one needs to write a corrective letter. I know that Al Gore did not invent the Internet although he once suggested he did. Nevertheless, I have been known to point out that God frequently speaks through Google (or Bing to be fair).

My fingers danced over the keys: "universities with online DNP programs." At that time, I found a list of seventeen universities that offered mostly online programs.

Chapter 7

University of Washington was not among them. I began at the top with one of Arizona's and then worked my way down the list looking at the programs and what would be required of me. One was quarterly classes for six quarters and a full week each quarter on campus. Six weeks of vacation or unpaid time off was not in the budget. Next. After looking over four or five of the schools and flipping past one university simply because I just didn't like the name, I clicked the next offering.

"Two days each semester for on-campus intensive" is what it read. What I read was "spend the weekend with us on campus." I clicked around further and fell in love with what I thought would be an easy-to-manage online program. Goal: find a reasonable DNP program to become a doctor. Plan: click around on the Internet until lunch.

Like I said, making plans can follow a myriad of forms. That day my goal changed and became more specific: Get my DNP from Duke University. Lucky for me the plan for admission to Duke was outlined and all I needed to do was follow the simple directions.

I had no idea where or what Duke University was or stood for. Oh sure, I had heard of it before; they had a number one basketball team, right? Like I followed basketball. I didn't realize the magnitude of what I was proposing to get myself into that day. I had no concept on that late morning, clicking around the Internet of the mountain I was actually looking to climb. Heck, I thought Raleigh-Durham was one long-named city. I remember flying through there when I was six years old because one of my mother's frequently told stories, I believe number fourteen, was about picking up our family's boat and getting snowed in on Easter Sunday in Newark. We had to start numbering the stories so we could just insert the number during dinner conversations to save the time rather than hearing it again.

It is a good thing that I didn't know the mountain I faced. Many times we plan and perceive the outcome as impossible or too difficult, and no matter what we say our plans are, what we really want to do is quit. How many times have you started something that you knew would be hard and as you worked, it became more challenging and difficult until you convinced yourself that the best thing would be to surrender and give up because it is obviously impossible? The energy around wanting to quit becomes all-encompassing and we find every reason to alter plans enough so that everything goes off the rails in order to look back and say, "See, that was an unrealistic dream." This is why your inventory is so important (see Chapter Four: Understanding your G.I.F.T.S.) You need to know where your foundational beliefs will take you and what threatens your progress in life. Take out your demons and shake them off and show them the light of day so that they don't change your plans and make you quit your dreams.

Take writing this book, for instance. I have been talking about it for years and the time has never been right (which it wasn't). Then when I start to move into my intentional process around its creation, I find myself surrounded by books written by other authors who I think are "much better" authors than I am. I realize that I have been duped again by my insecurities and the truth is that my story is vital and important and I am its author.

One of my favorite self-help authors, Dr. Wayne Dyer, says that he sits down on the beach in Maui with a stack of yellow pads and creates his books without editing. He writes stream of consciousness. Spirit is writing the books through him. I threw my pen down, "I can't do that," I complain. I sure can't with that attitude, would be my response. It is amazing how the conversation in my head can go from "Go, George, Go" to "You're boring; just quit now while you can." I guess it is time I made friends with the roommate in my head.

In his book, The *Untethered Soul*, Michael A. Singer does a marvelous job of breaking down the effects and patterns of self-talk that come from this "inner roommate." I find myself right back to that place of negative internal messaging as I am reading his book on changing this talk: "I could never write like this guy or present this information so concisely or beautifully." I find myself trying to undo my plans to write this book as a way to protect myself from … just what exactly? Singer writes, "True personal growth is about transcending that part of you that is not okay and needs protection." Time for true personal growth! Incidentally, we loved The *Untethered Soul* so much we gave it as a present to our entire wedding party.

I am so grateful to Michael Singer and Wayne Dyer and many wonderful authors like them. What I realize as I read books by these authors is that I can't write just like them, nor should I because then I would be them. They have helped me realize that it is my telling of my experience that is uniquely mine. Only I can describe my experience in a way that speaks to the people who will benefit from this book. Each of us has a unique experience with life that is so necessary, so important, and needs to be fulfilled for a greater purpose that has yet to be realized in common hours. I only have to write like Dr. George Baxter-Holder and no one else can. How great is that? That is your gift too. You can only do what you do as you and no one else can!

I wish that I only had to have one stern conversation with myself to stop the self-talk that would throw away all plans to write this book. The truth is it is a continual conversation that is full of love and acceptance for this process and this intention. My dream is to help people get past their limiting struggles and move into a life of celebration. My goal is to write this book as a catalyst of Spirit's teaching through me. My plan is to write one story at a time and seek out help and guidance to put it all together. One story at a time is EASY! I don't have to write a book; I just have to tell a story. I don't have to write it stream of consciousness in a week but I do have to write it consciously. Being conscious when it comes to plans means writing it down and creating it physically, even if you think you don't know what you are doing. There is a movement of energy that happens when you create that is indescribable. It is like taking all of the creative force that is found in the Universe and laser focusing it on your plan.

Remember, there is an inexhaustible supply of creative

Chapter 7

force so you are not taking anyone else's away. I love the Prosperity Plus teaching from Mary Manin Morrissey when she says that we give the Universe a check it can cash. Imagine a bank of creative yumminess in the Universe and all you have to do is write down what you need to withdraw from this bank and KABOOM, it is yours. If you go into a bank to cash a check without a check written out, just how much money do you think you will leave carrying from the bank?

I remember starting my aesthetics business, Seattle Youthful, in 2010. How easy it would have been to walk into a bank and cash a big check to get the business started. Unfortunately, without a plan, banks don't like handing out money. The business was originally named Youthful Aims. The name came to me without much careful planning (overstatement)—without any planning. I was actually looking for pictures for marketing Botox treatments and there was a picture with a woman's face with a target right between the eyebrows, the most treated area with Botox.

I thought the picture was perfect and would go great with the name Youthful Aims. Remember, lack of planning is also a plan. Failure to plan is planning to fail. I ran the name and logo past a few friends who generally said yes to me and, poof, a business was born.

From that point, I tried to make everything fit to the predetermined outcome. I was so attached to this thing I had birthed. I was coming up with tag lines to explain the picture and blog pieces that were coming to me in doodles. I had a logo that I dearly loved with a stylized "Y" with a heart in the center. I was very proud of my doodle design until someone said, "I didn't know if it were fallopian tubes or two hammers, and then I saw the heart. Oh, how cute." Remember that buzzer sound that went off in game shows when the contestants were wrong? That rang in my head.

I needed to make a change in my business model, name, logo, and direction. I needed to do branding. The whole thing sounded official and grown up. What I really needed was a plan. I needed to let go of attachments to the outcome and allow Spirit to guide my business in a new direction. What I had come to know in my process of growing up is that Spirit spoke through others around me and divine patterns would show up in the simplest of things.

My dear friend Barrie and I started to develop a new brand and plan for the business. I was so grateful to have someone in my life willing to help guide me in a new direction for the business. From this new branding and planning, Seattle Youthful was hatched. In my mind, the company was about capturing the essence of Youthful, and Seattle is where it started. It was about Transformative Medical Arts, changing and transforming lives to be a more authentic representation of the true nature of individual Spirit. It is my dream that this book and subsequent workshops are all a part of that process and healing.

I believe that there is a way that all of this could come to pass regardless of how well I planned. What I know is that there is no stopping the Universal drive to say yes to abundance and healing. As humans, we are spiraling upward toward a greater enlightenment in universal consciousness.

Chapter 7

In quiet moments, you can feel that this is true. Each of us needs to take time for these quiet moments, even if it is just five minutes a day, and do nothing.

There is a meditative practice that can help. I have used it and still come back to it because of its simplicity. Sit still in a room where you will have no distractions. The bathroom is always a reasonable choice although not as comfortable as some other rooms that come to mind. Light a candle and sit far enough away from the candle that your breath will have little effect on the flame. Set an alarm for the time that is comfortable to you. Stare into the heart of the flame and focus on the coolness of your breath as it goes in and out of your nostrils. Focus on nothing but the coolness. Breathe in, breathe out, and release any judgment you have about the thoughts that come to you. When you recognize a thought being stuck say to yourself on the in breath, "I accept this thought" and on the out breath, "I bless this thought." When the alarm goes off resume your day and see if there is a change in your consciousness.

Each of us can personally change our relationship with conscious thought in this way and be responsible for the fulfillment of a greater plan. We can participate collectively with each other to change consciousness by attending church, social gatherings, or political causes. However, it really just takes each of us quietly making the commitment to personally grow.

Take time to plan your life without attachment to the outcome. What steps are necessary for you to act on in the fulfillment of your dreams? If you could do one thing today that would move you closer to your personal heaven what would that one thing be? Write it down. Let the next indicated step flow naturally from that one thing and soon you will have a written plan for you to start Step Eight, Taking Action.

CHAPTER 8:

Taking Action

> *"In recovery we connect with reality through action. We show up and do our part.... We learn who we are by taking a stand, taking risks, and allowing ourselves to be vulnerable. Even when we make mistakes, we can learn something vital about ourselves."*
>
> **Narcotics Anonymous,** *Living Clean:*
> ***The Journey Continues***

Action is the key to all intentional living. It is with action that dreams and goals become realities. Without action, dreams are simply unrealized fantasies.

I remember that as a child when I wanted something I would just "go for it" and make it happen. Somewhere along the path in life, I bought and paid for insecurity and fear. I have no idea where they came from, but they were of the finest grade and purest quality, abject fear of everything. Unfortunately, it is not a unique story.

It is this unrealistic fear and insecurity that is the antidote to action. There is nothing more halting in the human condition than self-reflection through a broken lens. The cracks are self-doubt, insecurity, fear, and emotional pain, and they can skew the image until progress screeches to a stop. This is the good news and the bad.

What this means for your life is that you have the responsibility for life's progress. Personal responsibility takes over from blame and victimhood. Each action we take as humans is on purpose, ON PURPOSE!

"Separate the thinkers from the doers by their actions," I once wrote in my own journal. It seems like such a "duh" statement but it is so ripe with truth. I cannot tell you how much futile energy I have spent wanting and wishing for outcomes only to spend about half the energy on actually "doing." Writing this book has been a prime example of this and ironically, the most glaring manifestation has been this chapter on Action.

I get stuck in wanting the action to be perfect or I don't want to even start. I want the words to flow out of my pen and onto the page with exacting pentameter and have the reader lifted to new heights and carried to some faraway land of my twisted life. I am sure that I am not the only perfectionist out there that is completely paralyzed from taking action. Clearly, if you have no idea what I am talking about you might just want to skip to the next chapter on Celebration, because it is just more fun … for a time.

I get so stuck in wanting the action to be perfect. I will agonize for weeks maybe months, on what to say about taking action. The whole conundrum doesn't make logical sense. "Just write something!" I will scream at the perfectionist procrastinator in my head and "I will, but …" is the only response.

Imagine if every creative genius were paralyzed in this way. Michelangelo's *David* would be stuck in a block of marble with some pensive far-off gaze not wanting to have hands that were out of proportion. Beethoven might have

Chapter 8

petered out after the Fourth and never written the Fifth. Martin Luther King, Jr. might have had a dream, but kept it to himself for fear that no one would understand. I am NOT comparing the product of my work to the work of Michelangelo, Beethoven, or Dr. King, but creativity is creative energy and energy can neither be created nor destroyed, just harnessed, squelched, or set free. That energy is going to continue to exist somehow. It will make itself known either positively or negatively. Energy doesn't matter how it is expressed, just that it is. This became clearly evident in the darker times of my life.

I was not always paralyzed by the notion of perfection. Remember my snap decision to plan and execute the great goldfish heist? I don't remember spending much premeditated energy on not acting in that one. I probably should have but that is not the point.

Somewhere in life my impulsivity started to wane. I know that it was somewhere between fourth grade and forty. I became a compulsive overthinker. It came on slowly. It was presumably triggered by a decision or series of decisions that had undesired or unpredicted outcomes.

I remember in fourth grade, for instance, there were a few decisions made that stuck with me for a while. One of these is something I still do today although I am grateful for it.

Picture day in fourth grade was different for me. Maybe some pre-pubescent hormones kicked in around that time or maybe subconsciously, I had a schoolboy crush on my teacher, Mr. Romanelli. I remember always speaking up in class and was frequently looking to get attention from the teacher. They called me a class clown ... I knew what I was doing even then. Looking back on it now it is clear that I made no conscious decision to be gay unless that decision was made in third grade ... Actually, my third grade teacher was frightening and very witch-like, so maybe she did turn me gay, although I don't really think that is possible. Could have been worse, I suppose, she could have turned me into a newt, but I digress.

I was getting ready before school to pick the perfect outfit that would memorialize my time with Mr. Romanelli. I knew it had to be something distinctive that would stand out and make a bold statement. Although I gave solid consideration to my rainbow *Mork & Mindy* suspenders, I decided ultimately on a bow tie, simple, distinctive, and classy. That one quick decision and action lead to Mr. Romanelli giving me a pet name that stuck: George "Bow-Tie" Baxter. To this day, I love wearing my bow ties and have one for almost every occasion.

Other quick actions in fourth grade did not have the same impact on my future self. I recall being in music class and the band teacher was having us decide what instrument to play in band for the rest of our lives. This is a huge decision to make for a fourth grader and one that really needs to be more than a snap decision. Mr. Graham was the band director. His wife worked at a private school with my mother and they were all professionally immersed in music, so this decision was going to be an important one for me. Also, it was important, even in fourth grade, for people to like me and authority figures to recognize my uniqueness—a double-edged sword.

Had I actually taken the time to consider all of the ramifications of the "what instrument" decision, I would have brought to mind carrying the instrument home on the bus and storing it in my bedroom at home. I would have considered all of the possibilities for solo opportunities and the ability to shine and stand out. Had I thought about all of these things I would have selected the flute, oboe, clarinet, or trumpet. Heck, the drums only need sticks to tap on any number of things. But no, Mr. Graham said that the underdog of the band was the Baritone Horn.

"Not many people play it," he said.

In a flash, I took that to mean that rooting for the underdog could make me shine. That one snap decision and I was stuck with the second biggest instrument in the band sitting next to me on a lonely bus seat for eight more years: two presidential terms, more than half my life at that point. A lot can happen in a timeframe like that and yet I jumped right up and took action for the brass underdog without so much as a thought. Fast forward and I am agonizing how to put the right words together in the right order to ensure that people will be able to understand what I am trying to convey in this book. Perhaps more thought then and less now and I would be a bestselling author writing about my world tour playing the oboe.

The ability to take action can sometimes stem from a level of confidence. This becomes a catch-22 of sorts because I have defined "confidence" as something which comes from doing something again and again and becoming proficient at it or being born with an innate ability, like the art of bullshit, for instance. Are some people born with a bullshit gene? That would explain why some people flourish in sales or politics. It is also what allows people who suffer from low confidence to act in situations where there has been no direct experience. This innate ability to bullshit and take action saved my mother and me from being stuck in Barcelona one summer.

There are so many stories that morph into a tell-all memoir about an eighteen-year-old gay man coming of age in Europe with his mother, but this is neither the time nor the place. Let's just say that my ability to live a double life inside the confines of the United States was expanded on a three-week tour of Greece, Spain, Italy, and France.

As promised, my mother took me to Europe to show me the sights and culture, which we did by day. By night, I was shown the underbelly of Athens, Barcelona, Rome, Venice, and Paris by a handsome disc jockey from Mykonos, a male model from Milan, and others. I am quite certain that we saw and did things that are not found on any public tour of those cities. The underground catacombs have never been seen in such light, but I digress.

As far as languages were concerned, my mother and I divvied up the four countries; I took Italian and Spanish and she was responsible for Greek and French. I had taken three years of high school Spanish so I was not too concerned with my abilities to get by. This ability was put to the test, however, when we got to the airport in Barcelona.

Chapter 8

We were traveling "space-available" because my father worked for United Airlines. Back in 1983, United was a premier company and had a great working collaboration with many of the other airlines around the globe. We flew to Athens on World Airlines, which to this day holds my vote for the best flight and best service in the air. I am not sure if they are still in business but I hope they are. We flew on Iberia Airlines from Athens to Barcelona and we were supposed to continue on Iberia from Barcelona to Rome.

Sometime between my introducing myself to the Greek DJ on the nude beach in Aegina and sailing a sailboard out into the Mediterranean Sea without the skills to turn around, Iberia Airlines went on strike and shut down. We were in the dark until we arrived at the airport in Barcelona.

We had a problem and it was time for some action. We knew that goal was to get off the Iberian Peninsula and hopefully over to the boot of Italy. There was no travel agent to call and no 1-800 numbers to dial. These are the luxuries you give up when you fly on free passes. You are basically freeloading on the kindness of foreign air carriers who may or may not like Americans but have some working relationship with United Airlines, which they call reciprocity. I am not sure how, but I came up with the Spanish word for "reciprocity" and just in the nick *del tiempo*.

I sprang into action when we found ourselves stuck by looking at the "Departures" board and all of the Iberia flights were listed as "Cancelled." There is a sinking feeling—struggle. Take stock in the situation—surrender. Know that you are going to get out of Barcelona—belief.

Imagine a different travel plan—dream. Get to Italy—goal. Find other flights to Rome—plan. Argentina Airlines—action. Finding the word for "reciprocity"—priceless.

I checked the departure board for another flight to Rome and saw that there was one on an airline that was listed as "AA." Being the fine American boy that I am, I assumed it was American Airlines. Why do fine Americans assume so much? My mother tried to dash this plan with the news that she was certain that American does NOT have reciprocity with United. Thank God that AA can mean different things to different countries. A quick review of the Airline codes at Aeropuerto de Barcelona and I discovered AA stood for Argentine Airlines. I told my mother to wait there and I went to find the ticket desk "just to see" what they might be able to do for us in Argentina.

I walked up to the ticket counter being manned by a very handsome Latin man and explained our predicament. He tapped away on the keyboard for a bit while I searched my mental Spanish dictionary for the right thing to say. Thank God for cognates, words that sound the same in English and Spanish: *reciprocidad*. I asked in Spanish, "Con aerolina United?" "Oh, Si," was the response. If ever I question my belief in a power in the Universe that brings people and situations together at the absolutely perfect time I just recall what happened next.

For whatever political reason, Argentina Airlines is able to stop in Barcelona and let passengers from Buenos Aires deplane, before continuing onto Rome. However, they are not permitted to allow new paying passengers on to

Chapter 8

continue to Rome. Luckily for me and my mother this meant that there were plenty of seats available and we were not paying passengers. Thank God for freeloading.

I hurried back to where my mother was sitting with our bags. The handsome Latin AA desk agent followed me over to my mother and stood by my side. My mother looked at me apprehensively with that "What did you do now?" look. I explained that we were going to fly from Barcelona to Rome on Argentina Airlines but that we had to hurry because the plane was leaving in a few minutes and this nice man needed to walk us to the plane. I told her that we have reciprocity with Argentina Airlines and she looked shocked. She had a proud spring in her step as we hurried out to the plane. The Latin desk hunk carried my mother's bag for her because that is what Latin desk hunks do and off we went to Rome.

We settled into our seats and tried to catch our breath. I remember sitting in silence for a bit while we taxied and took off. Sometime after takeoff, my mother turned to me and smiled. "How on earth did you come up with the word for 'reciprocity'?" she asked proudly. I don't know, mom. It just came to me. I guess bullshit is bilingual and action translates into any language.

The contrast to taking hero-like action in life is getting caught up in an action spiral full of shame and discontent. How many times growing up did my mother or father say, "Why did you do that?" only for me to assume a posture of the sweetest innocence, hoping their incredulous anger might be melted by my childlike cuteness. I remember really not knowing why I did this or that thing that invariably hurt me or someone else or at least put someone in grave danger. Perhaps, it was the danger.

What could be more dangerous than hanging out with two drunken drag queen prostitutes? Well, plenty of things I am certain, but I remember this is where I found myself on one occasion.

I was driving my 1978 Mercedes-Benz 300 up to Vancouver, British Columbia on a warm summer day in 1992. In the front seat was Queeny (*aka* Mark) and in the back seat was Debra (*aka* Ed). While these are not their real names, no innocence is being protected.

What stands out still is how fun these two spirits were. I remember laughing: deep, genuine, belly laughter. The kind that makes your face feel like it went to the gym. These two could get me laughing about just anything. I was equally fascinated when they would talk about men and money.

With the exception of very prominent Adam's apples, these two were each very convincing women and would get men to part with hundreds of dollars while they proved what talented women they were. I was truly amazed that the men were never the wiser. The physics alone perplexed me, but I guess men willing to pay for coitus don't mind only spooning.

On the way up to Vancouver, the Benz was renamed Miss Sadie Benz and both Queeny and Debra regaled us stories of their exploits with nasal falsetto. They also taught me how I could also make some "hard" earned cash in

Chapter 8

Canada. They explained men to me in a way that was both intriguing and dangerous. Men, straight or gay, are willing to pay to have their needs and desires met. If you have not already realized, this is where the story might get too vivid for some. For others, you know who you are; it might not be vivid enough. Mom, if you are actually reading this … just skip ahead a few pages for your own sake.

I was fascinated by these two individuals. I could not understand how face-to-face these two could thoroughly convince men they were women. When I say thoroughly convince, I mean from beginning to happy ending, from "how do you do?" to "show me the money." Intelligent, semi-intelligent, or not-so-intelligent men never the wiser having just had what they thought was the usual run-of-the-mill fornication albeit with back entry only. None of them seemed to know that they were in the way back. I was shocked.

I had been running a successful escort agency in Seattle for several months in the early 1990s cleverly named "Architects of Intrigue" with my friend Steve, and that seemed exciting and dangerous all on its own. This face-to-face, on the fly, pay for sex business took the cake. I advertised in the *Gay Times* newspaper, which made business pretty easy. Customers were pre-screened by picking up that paper. They were gay, bisexual, or just freaky enough to be interesting.

It was a peculiar little business that Steve and I ran; and no, that was not his real name. Men would call and we would give them a choice of six different "types" like tall,

Italian, and handsome, or sporty and athletic, etc. After a conversation on the phone, Steve and I would decide which of us fit their "type." Depending on who was most likely their type, the other of us would meet them to get their information and make sure they were not law enforcement. It was exciting and dangerous and satisfied many of my addictive needs at the time. This was the daily action that I was taking to live to my fullest, I thought. I had no idea how stuck I was.

None of that compared to this newly discovered danger. I was the observer of these men (or women) in action and I was in awe. They would have me drive Miss Sadie Benz slowly down a crowded Vancouver street as men were walking from bar to bar in a relatively blue-collar neighborhood. They told me what we were doing was called "trolling," like for fish, only different bait. Every so often one or the other of them would yell out the car window in their nasal falsetto that sounded more like a goose protecting a nest than a woman of the night, "Hey baby, wanna date?' It was something right out of a candid camera episode and I was howling with laughter.

I was howling right up until Mark jumped out of the car at a stop light and was off with some rough-looking longshoreman type. "Is he going to be okay?" I asked Ed.

"Girl, don't even worry about her, girl, she can take care of herself. We meet back up at the hotel in a couple hours or so. Don't you worry. It is time for us to get our tricks."

I guess up until that point I didn't realize we were actually in the Action step. I thought we were just playing, plotting,

Chapter 8

planning. Just having fun. I realized at that moment that this was a job, a quest, an opportunity, and dangerous.

We parked the car and set out on foot. We were in one of those neighborhoods that blends over into the next like the intersection of circles in a Venn diagram. We were at the intersection of "Collar (blue)" and "Flag (rainbow)." We were right where we were supposed to be.

We walked into a dark bar and it was as I expected—the intersection. Everyone dressed blue collar but on the weekends played in rainbow. This was the weekend Perception shapes our experience of events and situation. I walked into this bar, a committed gay man, yet far from flamboyant. At my side was a very flamboyant, nasal-honking drag queen who continued to keep me belly laughing. However, what all the blue color studs in the bar saw walk in was a tall, dark, handsome curious straight man with his black girlfriend. In an instant, I went from predator to prey; remember it is all about perception. The hunted are so vulnerable when they think they are the hunter.

We started drinking and chatting up the men in this bar. It wasn't long before Debra and I were sitting back to back talking to separate, yet interested men. Every so often I would catch a laugh and a goose honk from behind me and I knew it would not be long before I would be left all alone to fend for myself in this dangerous place. Wink, wink. I had every confidence in Debra's skill to leave me alone.

She got suddenly quiet and I turned to see the profile of a longshoreman tragically lacking finesse while attempting to eat Debra's face. They stayed locked like that for a few

Drugs, Food, Sex and *God*

more moments and then carried on some hushed conversation that I am certain was about money and where they could go. Our hotel room was off-limits.

I carried on my conversation with this guy Tim, kind of a shy geeky type looking for just about anything. We talked for a while longer as we both noticed the pair behind us leaving. Tim seemed surprised and excited that I just waved as my girlfriend left me for another man. He immediately changed his demeanor and even in his drunken state could tell he was that much closer to getting lucky.

We finished our drinks and Tim leaned with a whisky whisper to tell me to follow him to the bathroom. Acting drunker than I was, I followed, but had no intention of being put in a position without any means of easy escape. Danger is one thing but being reckless is just stupidity. We walked back toward the bathrooms and I pulled Tim into a phone booth in the dark hallway leading to the back. It was a cramped space but perfect for what had to be done.

Tim's pants easily slid to the floor weighed down with his belt and heavy wallet. I had no conversation with Tim about an exchange of pleasure for money although I knew there would be such an exchange. It was there in that cramped booth that I went into action to get paid like my prostitute drag queen friends had instructed me to do. As Tim was distracted in that phone booth I reached around his feet on the floor and found his fat wallet, which I immediately emptied of its paper contents, then put it back in his pants. I have always been skilled at multi-tasking. Working hard behind the scenes while keeping people happy and well

Chapter 8

served up front is something I learned in the restaurant business and I was just putting my skills to work again with a slightly different twist.

Tim was spent and drained of his energy and money although he would not realize the latter until I was long gone. The feeling was a rush like getting high for the first time. At that moment, I found out what addiction to adrenaline is all about. I hurried down the street and doubled back a few times to make sure that Tim would never find me.

As the adrenaline started to wear off and remorse was tickling the back side of my consciousness, I knew I needed to go back to the hotel and get high, really high. Facing what I had actually done without the numbing salve of the needle was more than I could take. It became the only way I could deal with who I had become. The higher I got, the more normal I felt that I became and the less normal I actually was—a conundrum.

Taking action is a critical step in really living life. It is actually the living step. There is no life without it. You can't hope, trust, or wish it so. You can dream and plan but if you don't actually do something, your beingness will never be actualized.

Taking action as a result of peer pressure can have disastrous effects. Taking action that is contrary to your beingness becomes a wooden shoe in the machine of life, the very definition of sabotage. You start sabotaging your life and don't even realize it because you are surrounded by people you identify with as friends doing what they do. The perception and lens of your life changes, not because you change on any deep character level, but because what is right and normal changes. Wars and atrocities are committed with this same mind-set.

For me, I found myself on my knees robbing some man too ecstatic to care because I was a junkie who succumbed to peer pressure. It was in succumbing that I took my action, a life action that doesn't look like much on the outside but rots you from the inside.

Let me be clear—not all peer pressure is bad or fruitless. It is all dependent upon the peers, their actions, and how that fits with your internal code of right and wrong. It is not my job to judge whether sexual extortion of longshoremen in Canada is right or wrong for all, just if it works for me in the long term. Clearly, it served a purpose in the short term.

Once I got off drugs, my peers changed, my priorities changed, my dreams, goals and plans all changed. There was a vacuous sense of regret and remorse that I knew I had to deal with and still deal with today. Once my head was clearing, I knew that I could get on with my life and become the man I always wanted to be. I could celebrate the man Carol Baxter wanted me to be.

CHAPTER 9:

CELEBRATION

"Choose to be in close proximity to people who are empowering, who appeal to your sense of connection to intention, who see the greatness in you, who feel connected to God, who live a life that gives evidence that Spirit has found celebration through them."
Wayne Dyer

If I had known this particular weekend in July 2000 would be my last big meth hurrah I would have done nothing differently. When an addict starts to use drugs frequently, you hear that they are always "chasing that first high." Some addicts die chasing that feeling. There is no timetable, no schedule of events; everything is quite random and alarmingly variable.

There is no way for a using addict to know or control whether they will be one of the rare few fortunate ones who will experience anything as devastatingly wonderful as the first high. More often than not, the using addict simply sinks to the bottom of the pond in life and bumps along aimlessly, destroying family relationships, personal well-being, career (if it still exists), health, and overall sanity. There are also those few committed using addicts who die chasing that first one. What a struggle for the using addict, wanting to die, having the means, and not succeeding. Looking for an easy way out of a feeling and winding up desperately seeking a better life.

It occurs to me that not everyone is this type of desperate, degraded, hopeless drug addict. Addicts come in all shapes, sizes, ages, demographics, and backgrounds. The story I have to tell is my story and I was a desperate, hopeless, down-in-the-gutter or under-a-bush type addict willing to sell my soul (or yours) for my drugs and my way out. I love it when people tell me, "But you don't look like an addict." There is a look to hopelessness but drugs of all varieties offer the addict a mask to cover the hopelessness.

My first day without the use of any mind or mood-altering substances was Saturday, July 8, 2000, I think. That was the day that I told my probation officer it was, but during that time in my life, lying was almost second nature. I do know two things: if it was not that day it was very close to it and for more than fourteen years I have been celebrating that day as "the" day. I picked that day and I kept that day. This was the day my new life really began, a birthday of sorts. It was a day when peace took hold in my life. It was a day of celebration of ending and beginning. It was the perfect last step in my downward spiral and the perfect first step up out of the gutter.

So my first day clean was July 8, 2000, but I was discharged from prison on February 8, 2000. A lot of things happened in those five months. While I was given a second chance on February 8, I didn't take it. I was released to Community Custody to be paroled to Scott, my community corrections officer. Many of Scott's parolees were repeat offenders or soon to be. He either recognized that I might be different or wished that it were so. Either way I had an uncanny ability to bullshit, especially when my life and freedom depended on it. Ours was a professional relationship between officer and felon. I would tell him what he wanted to hear and he would watch me pee in a cup.

Clearly, using drugs was against my parole agreement and I did really well with this for a long time after I was released. I believe that it was ten days to be exact! I used with some friends on February 18, a friend's birthday. It was a Friday and I was sure that I would not be letting Scott watch me pee in a cup for at least three days. Three days is the time the Internet claims it takes for meth to get out of your system. I took it to be fact.

Random urinalysis (UA) works like this: you have a color assigned to you. Mine was ironically yellow. You call in to an automated system each day and if your color is up for that day then you had until the end of the business day to present yourself and pee in a cup for the nice man. Random being, well random … it was unlikely that the color would come up twice in a week or two days in a row for that matter. What are the odds? It was a chance I was willing to take like spinning a roulette wheel. When you are bumping along the bottom in life, your risk profile looks markedly different. Actually, just considering the actual odds of my color coming up twice in a row put me ahead of the class in Scott's roster of felons. Most drug addicts would act first and try and talk their way out of it. I wanted to be different.

If avoiding a "dirty" UA was being good, then I was being pretty good for months, five to be exact. Looking back on it, I am lucky that it was only five months because it could have been much worse. Using drugs against your will like that is the definition of a "slippery slope." I had a foolproof system and as long as I stopped in time for the meth to clear my system before my next UA, I would be home "free." Every time! The irony of thinking this was freedom is amazing.

It was the week of July 4, 2000 and I am not certain where my partner at the time was, but he was out of town. The holiday was a Tuesday that year and a mid-week holiday meant that government types would not be working as much or as hard that week. Nevertheless, I knew I could not get high on the Fourth of July as my color could come up the next day. I did go to work on July 5 and was called in for a UA that day. I think we all were. Scott got to watch a lot of felons pee that day. The chances of coming back again that week were so slim that I thought I would just give myself a bit of a holiday for the rest of the week. Partner out of town, peed in a cup on Wednesday, off work Thursday and Friday; it all was a perfect setup for what would be my last hurrah. I knew I could use on Thursday and Friday and still have the meth out of my system if my color came up the next week. I chased my first high those next two days and being exceptional and rare, I was able to catch it and experience it again and walk away.

Everything was as I wanted those two days. I went over to my dealer's apartment on Capitol Hill in Seattle on Thursday and did not leave for two days. His name was also George and he was attractive in that "I have free drugs" kind of way. Because of what he did for a living people wanted to be his friend and hang out with him. They would also do

Chapter 9

just about anything he asked to get what they wanted, poor people. It is only in hindsight that I realize I was just one of those people, prostituting myself for dope.

The drugs had their desired effect and I was in a state of ecstasy that I had not felt since my first time using meth in 1992. I needed to frontload my dope because I had a UA next week and needed everything out of my system by Monday the tenth. That was my rationalization.

There was a seeming parade of cute boys who came to the apartment during a span of time that seemed to stand still. Some stayed a little while and some stayed for longer depending on their level of commitment and desperation. None of it mattered to me because I had become a fixture on the couch desperately lost in my disease and time slipped away. I remember talking to a young man named Puppy, although I don't know why he was named that. I had talked to him before and thought that he was a straight boy. He was not straight that day.

My mind was a blur of euphoria, desperation, degradation, superiority, and insecurity. It was a bitter mind-soup that slowly blended together into one batch of remorse. When I finally realized where I was, it was early in the morning on Saturday, July 8. There was a feeling that came over me that I can only describe as peace. I felt complete somehow. I felt drained of my downward seeking and of all of my hopelessness. In their place was hope. If I had known then what I know now, I would have said that I felt the hand of God on my shoulder gently nudging me out of that apartment and on with my life.

George walked me out, perhaps as a way of temporarily

escaping the throes of chaos that had become his home. I think that at some level I had become some kind of grounding force for him, at least over the last two days. We made small talk in the elevator as the car descended to the lobby. When the doors opened out on a sunlit dawn, I turned and faced him. "Thank you, George. This has been an amazing two days for me and I don't believe that I will ever see you again." I was sure of it and he could tell it was the truth. I don't know why I was so sure, but deep within my being I felt it profoundly. Perhaps it was my confidence in my perfect system to beat the UA testing.

Two days later, I had my first dirty UA.

Celebration is that step of the intention process that seems like a no-brainer. Your life works out as you have planned and directed and you are happy enough to kick up your heels and make merry. Wrong. Celebration is the act of marking one's pleasure at a given time point related to a particular goal, but it also is a time of reflecting back on this process. It also is the space where those areas of struggle can show up.

Remember we are not dealing with a linear process or even a cyclical process although it tends to be more cyclical then linear. It actually looks more like a spider web of connection between all points; however, each step must be passed in order around one particular aspect of life. If life were one thing at a time, it would look more like a perfect circle. The fact is, we get challenged constantly in the areas of wealth, health, relationships, and creative expression and have the opportunity to be anywhere on the cycle in any area at any time.

Chapter 9

The completion step of celebration is where you invite your community to share in your joy. Your friends, family, and sphere of influence get to share in your lessons and encounters. This time not only marks your arrival at a desired spot but also can inspire others to dream, set goals or take action as they have witnessed in your life.

I can't tell you how many times I have watched the Academy Awards and been inspired to get back into acting. "Someday, I will win an Oscar," I would think. Off I would go and get another set of headshots, audition for a bunch of unpaid film work to put on my resume, look for an agent, have a great time, but still not get a nomination. I have actually stopped watching the Oscars because it makes my life too complicated and costs me too much money.

Remember, my whole premise is that this step-wise approach to intention works forwards or backwards. You can use intention to spiral your life upwards the same way you can also use intention to spiral out of control downward. When you set an intention of total demise and chaos in your life and you reach your intended goal, you are also in celebration, although you probably don't call it that. However, you have marked your desired completion of your intention.

It may seem odd that getting a dirty UA after prison or using drugs in prison was a celebration; however, it was a pinnacle in a very inverted sort of way. I was able to use that time in a bathroom stall as a moment of reflection on my journey to that point and ask, "So where shall I go from here?" Remember, it was at that point when my spiral stopped spinning down and the cycle began spinning the other way.

There have been so many things in my life to celebrate and I continue to be grateful for new and wonderful celebrations. There will never be a celebration as huge for me as the day that I met my husband, Travis.

It was a visual thunderclap! A feeling that to describe it would only limit it. I was engulfed with my destiny in the blink of my eyes and a beat of my heart.

It was January 2, 2011 and I remember it like it was yesterday. It was the day my life blossomed into the glorious bloom that it is today. There are not many days that I remember so vividly, so completely, prior to that day. Many times, it seems as though my life has simply been a string of feelings that were only punctuated by a clock to represent a day.

I was at a party with a friend celebrating the twenty-fifth sober anniversary of another friend. To say I was with a friend is woefully understating my reality. I was actually with my boyfriend at the time. Let's just call him, Jay.

Jay and I started dating around September or October of the previous year, a remarkably long three or four months. We had known each other or known of each other for a very long time. The notion of "knowing of each other" is very prevalent in the gay community. It is really just symbolic of possibly seeing each other at a bar or bathhouse and ultimately not being that into it. I guess it is not really fair to say that we were not that into it in the past; neither of us was in any condition to assess what we were or were not that into.

Chapter 9

Bottom line: I am intensely grateful for that relationship with Jay. I learned a lot about myself and a lot about living with intention in the area of relationships. I found myself at home alone a lot while dating Jay because it seemed like he did not prioritize spending time with me. I used that time to get deeper into my meditative practice. What came from that was a very specific list of what I was looking for in a mate and what I expected from a relationship.

I remember sitting on the couch one night in Jay's apartment as he was telling me about talking with one of his clients. The client was joking with Jay about relationships that begin around the holidays and end on January 2. I remember being struck by the lack of humor of this story, particularly because I was trying so desperately hard to make this relationship fit into my vision of things. Relationships should never feel forced or like that much work. If Jay had only told me the story once, I might have written it off as a mildly amusing off-putting joke. But the story came up three different times and ultimately was set as destiny. For that, I thank God.

We went to that party together and I remember talking to some of Jay's friends toward the beginning of the party, when I truly believed that our relationship was going to end that day. It was not more than twenty minutes later that Travis walked in front of me and my entire beingness changed forever.

Now don't get me wrong. Travis and I were not even introduced that day, and there was no contact between us. After all, I thought I was still trying to make the relationship work with Jay. Ironically, a picture surfaced after the party of Travis looking off to the left and I just happen to be at the buffet looking to the right and it looks as though our eyes are meeting. I love that picture and truly see Spirit in that shot.

Jay and I finally broke up about ten days later with irreconcilable differences about what a continued relationship would mean for us. For once, I was clear about what I wanted in a relationship and Jay was clear he was not able to meet me where I was.

I was basking in the uncomfortable stew of bachelorhood for about a month. I dated a few people and realized quickly they did not fit my list. One night I received the most polite private message on Facebook. "Hi there, do you think we could be Facebook friends?" wrote Travis. "Absolutely" was my only reply and I sent him a friend request. That was February 17, 2011.

I remember we exchanged phone numbers so that we could call or text regarding having coffee sometime in the near future. I also remember thinking that there was something different about this guy, but I had thought that many times before and had yet to be right. There was always a first time.

I was on a trip visiting a friend in Los Angeles for the weekend, but kept texting with Travis. My friend was exhausted about hearing about Mr. Right (whom I had never formally met). We went to a meditation group on Saturday night and we sat silently for about twenty minutes and then wrote about what we got from our meditation. Again,

Chapter 9

Mr. Right was coming up through my mediation as well. "Make a date, already" was my poor, exhausted friend's advice. We arranged to meet on February 22, when I got back from L.A.

We met for coffee. That is a trick I learned early on in my dating life. Just in case you need a quick and clean out, meet first for coffee and you can always bail before you get committed to dinner or longer. We got our coffees and sat across from each other at a table and started to ask each other the obligatory first-date questions. Honestly, I don't remember much of what was said because I had this voice screaming at me in my head. "This is THE ONE, pay attention." Just to be sure, I suggested that we walk up the street to get dinner.

I wish I were one of those people who remembers every detail of a first date, like what each of us ate or what he was wearing but again all I could focus on was the beautiful and sweet gentle man in front of me and the insistent screaming voice in my head making sure I didn't mess this up.

The point of the story is that I listened to the voice and I celebrated the nudge from Spirit. I had been waiting for the perfect relationship to manifest in my life and it was through the process and steps of intention that I was aware and open to it showing up. I could detail how just in this one area of my life I went through all of the steps of intention to get to this point of celebrating this moment but that is a topic for a whole separate book.

This story would not be complete if I did not talk about

Drugs, Food, Sex and *God*

the weekend in May 2012 when I had two name changes. It started on a stage in Durham, North Carolina. "I present to you Dr. George Lytton Baxter III" was the announcement from the podium. It was like a volcano finally blew that had been bubbling for some time. Through trials, tribulations, tests, and papers I had finally become a Doctor. There are no adequate words to describe the feeling that I had at that moment. Consider the most beautiful flower in a field growing directly out of a big pile of cow manure ... that might be the feeling. I was that flower. I was the phoenix rising from the ashes. My life at that moment graduated to a new vista and I was transformed.

In the moment, all I was doing was sitting on a stage with a bunch of other professional nurses wearing big puffy blue gowns and blue hats. It looked like a Smurf convention. All of the transformation was happening on a spiritual plane. Some describe this on the inside but in actuality, it is all around us. When a life is transformed, all lives are transformed. That was the case that day, May 13, 2012, in that auditorium.

The Convocation planning committee asked me to be the Convocation Speaker and deliver a message to all of the nurses in that room that would catapult them to their greatness. I have no idea whether my message did any catapulting but I did challenge the whole room to be that one nurse who makes a difference in that one life. I believe that challenge to be true for all of us. Make your life matter by making your life matter. This takes intention and attention. To be clear, I am not talking about writing

Chapter 9

your vulnerable life story out in a two-hundred-plus page book for the world to read and share, although if that is your thing, GO FOR IT. I am talking about everything, each thing, even what you might consider the small things. Smile to the beautiful person in the checkout line at the grocery. Say "Thank you" to the person you talk to at the utility company. Hold a door open for the person behind you through every door. Be a shoulder to cry on, an ear to listen, or a kind word that is spoken. Do these things and your life will be transformed.

It is ironic that I was asked to speak at convocation and given a microphone and a captive audience the same week North Carolina voted to ban same sex marriage. I wanted to regale the audience with how stodgy and conservative a view that was. I wanted to tell them all that if they felt their marriage would be threatened by allowing gay marriage then one of them might be gay. I wanted to scream at them and tell them how wrong they were. I wanted to tell them how happy I was that I had found love and how dare they try to limit me and the love that I had for Travis. Instead, I spoke about hope, love, and empowerment. That day, I was that one nurse. Over the next two days, I changed my name again.

After I graduated from Duke, Travis and I flew to New York City to get married. We actually would not have gotten married in North Carolina even if it had been legal. Not because we have anything against the Tar Heel State, although "Tar Heel" does not have a pretty ring to it. We had planned all along to be married in my "home" state. I had developed messages of despair about the future of my happiness in New York and I would undo those messages with a beautiful "I do." We got our marriage license in the Marriage Bureau in Manhattan in front of a very dramatic Justice of the Peace and a group of dear friends. It was the right thing to do. Eventually, all people in our world will have that same right and be able to celebrate happiness.

This process of intention is cyclical, as I have pointed out previously; therefore, with celebration comes struggle. I was joyfully celebrating the culmination of the nine steps in finding someone to be in an intimate relationship with but now find myself in that space of wondering what our lives will be like, how will we build our family, how will we grow old without looking like it … struggle, again. This time, very intentionally.

CHAPTER 10:

WITH FIRM INTENTION

"Now, with firm intention, make a choice to no longer be that person, and let the energy of your decision become an experience that is unforgettable and allow it to begin to rewrite the programs. Make the choice a memorable experience."
Dr. Joe Dispenza

My life up to this point has been a memorable experience. The choices I have made along the way have made it possible for me to be right here, right now. I don't find myself wandering too far into the "what ifs" because none of that matters. It only takes me out of the present moment and sets me into some parallel universe where I am either too big or too small in relative proportion to who I am right now. The journey of this book has been a catharsis of sorts and, in conclusion, I see how my life can be used as a model of hope for anyone who may be struggling with limiting self-talk whether it is obvious like drugs, food, or sex, or more subtle like unworthiness or people-pleasing.

When I look back on my life, it has been a perfect straight line guided by a Spirit and a presence that has always been available to me. If I had never used drugs, food, or sex to fill the spiritual void inside I would not be the man I am today. I would not have my message to share. My message is that there is hope. No matter how far you feel you have strayed from your path in life, you can get back to living and choose differently for yourself. Your story does not need to be the same as mine. You don't need to go to prison or stick a needle in your arm for relief from the horror of life. You might just be unhappy and want something different but don't know what that is. This process can help. Be intentional about moving your life forward and you will move in the direction of your dreams, even the dreams yet to be dreamt.

When I look back on my life, I find that my struggles can be reduced to three main things. I always wanted to reach my potential but did not know what that meant. I struggled to come to some revelation about my sexuality and move into a place of self-love that allowed me the freedom to express myself with authenticity and integrity. Finally, I struggled, and still do at times, with being recognized and loved as a perfect, whole spiritual being. What I have come to in my life is that all of these things, all of these struggles, are internal. There is no need or benefit to look anywhere but within for the answers.

Every relationship, every situation, and every idea that I have in my life is an opportunity to hold up a mirror to my soul to find out what it is that I truly believe about myself. I can struggle. That is an option for me. It is not a requirement for my life and is not a necessity for my happiness. Today, I struggle with things that I consider luxurious problems. Who will I get to help me with my social media? How can I find time to take my puppies to the park with my very full life? What is the best way to make sure that Travis knows he is the most valuable player in my life and I adore him?

Chapter 10

These struggles are light years away from those of my past. What will it take to get my father to love and accept me as a gay man? How will I ever succeed in life with a criminal background? How do I get to my coffee without shooting up methamphetamines? These seem so far away. And I know that it could only take one bad decision to make them my future. It is through living with intention that I keep that future from being mine. It is through living with intention that you can keep that future from being yours, too. Today my struggles are wonderful and joyful opportunities to grow into an even better person.

Surrendering into each day, I allow life to flow easily and effortlessly. I live today like the Borg from Star Trek. "Resistance is futile." No truer words were ever spoken. I know that when I feel pain, pressure, frustration, or anger it is because I am resisting something. I am not going with the flow. To be clear though, I am not a victim to life. I remember river rafting when I was younger. Rafting is all about going with the flow. Fighting the current was almost impossible and virtually unwinnable, but when I was "in the flow," I really was able to steer my boat where I wanted, except upstream. This is the surrender I am talking about here. Living with intention is about surrendering to the winning side and guiding life in the direction of your dreams. Your dreams, not someone else's. What would life be like if you surrendered to it? What if Life, or God, or Spirit was out there for your Good? What if there was a conspiracy afoot to catapult you to your perfection? Would you surrender? Would you say, "Okay, God, you got me?

Take me in and make me perfect. I surrender?" I would now, but that is only after a half-life of fighting tooth and nail against an unseen force that I thought wanted to "get" me.

I remember sitting in court knowing that I was guilty. I turned to my public defender, who was just doing his job, and asked if there was any way to fight this. He said there was and I committed to fighting some more. I committed to resisting some more. I committed actually to three more active years of intravenous drug use, degradation, despair, and a life of total and complete chaos. I didn't know it at the time but resistance was futile. I was arguing for my limitations. I was battling for the bottom of my life instead of fighting to the top. Had I just said, "I surrender," it would have been a different experience. Again, the experience was necessary for my story to be complete.

Perhaps, through my experience with not surrendering you do not have to repeat my experience. Is there something that has your attention and about which you could just say, "I surrender?" What would life be like then? Do you believe that life could be even better?

It really is as you believe. All of the great sages, mystics, and teachers have said these exact words or ones just like them. Life can be what you make it. Getting a grasp on belief is as important as getting a grasp on reality. Actually, I think that they are one and the same. Your grasp on your beliefs can define your reality; I know it has mine.

When I was a young boy, I believed that I could do anything I wanted in life. I felt powerful and invincible.

Chapter 10

Something happened along the way that changed that feeling. I don't know what that thing was and don't really care, because knowing that thing is ultimately irrelevant. I needed to get back that feeling. Unfortunately, in my quest to find a new way to feel, I found drugs instead. The feeling was changed and I once again felt invincible. Sometimes I even felt superhuman; the feeling was not genuine. I had lost touch with my Spirit by using drugs, sex, food, and people to fill up the spiritual vacuum that was left inside. I needed to believe again.

They told me to find a Higher Power. They told me to make it anything I wanted and this was an easy task. Higher Power is everywhere. Clouds, tides, wind, electricity, even the weird little well of emotion that happens when someone tells you that you need to love and respect yourself are ways that a power greater than me shows up. Sometimes I hate it when emotion takes over in the middle of something important, like public speaking. Now, having surrendered to that, I usually prepare my audience to have tissues ready, not for them but for me.

Do you want to believe in a Higher Power, God, Spirit, or Universal Presence? If you don't, that's okay. It is not like there is anything that will happen to the Universe if you don't believe. The planets will stay aligned, I am pretty sure. Ask yourself though, How does that happen? How is it that billions of cells are cobbled together to form the human being and that the process seems to get repeated pretty well over seven billion times just for the ones still living? If you are open to this kind of belief, then get quiet and look inside through contemplation or meditation. If you want, use the affirmation that is at the beginning of this book as a starting point.

Practice believing in yourself by believing in other people. Find people you admire and watch what they do. Then try and emulate what they do. In Twelve Step recovery, this is done through sponsorship. I wish that everyone had a sponsor. Life would be so much easier. What if you had someone who truly believed in you and you admired and believed in them and you talked to them every day? How would that make your life different? Could you believe in yourself if they told you how amazing you truly are? Would you? There does not have to be overblown ego attached to recognizing your splendor. You do something amazingly well or you could, right? What if you looked at your reflection in the mirror every morning and found one positive thing to say to yourself about who you are. You don't have to get all Stuart Smalley, from *Saturday Night Live*, about it but if you want to borrow his line, "I am good enough, I am smart enough, and doggone it people like me." There is nothing wrong with speaking kindly to yourself. I need to constantly remind myself of this practice.

If you talked to me like I talk to myself sometimes, I would never have anything to do with you. If you abused me like I have abused myself, I would probably call the police. Don't be your own abuser. Don't punish yourself for not believing in yourself. Instead, find something to believe in. This takes intention.

It also takes really understanding your G.I.F.T.S. What

Chapter 10

makes you grateful? Insecure? What are your Foundational Values and what Threatens your progress? I am grateful for my life, my path, my husband, my career, and my friends. I know I am grateful for a whole mess of other things too but you get the point. Start every day with gratitude. Here is an exercise that I have my people that I sponsor do. Wake up in the morning and while you are lying in bed open your eyes and out loud say, "Today will be exceptional." Conversely, you could say, "Today is going to suck." Either way you are closer to your truth. Then when your right foot hits the ground say "Thank" and when your left hits say "You." Then you have quite simply started your day with, and in, gratitude. You could walk through the whole house like that saying, "Thank You, Thank you, Thank You."

Say thank you too for the things that make you insecure. I am so grateful that I know what makes me insecure because one of the things is that I think my writing sucks. But here I am writing anyway. Don't let your insecurities keep you from your joy and splendor. I have a friend who is insecure in crowds of people, but every time he goes to a party or event, he has a great time. He knows that he is insecure around these situations but he goes anyway and has a blast.

These things do not have to keep you stuck. If you are insecure about things that are changeable then take the action to change them. I remember early in recovery people would comment that I looked pregnant because I had gotten so fat in prison. I was very insecure about my weight and wore big baggy clothes to hide what I had become.

It was not until I actually took the step to do something about it that I could stop hiding. I remember the feeling I had when I could actually wear clothes that fit and even form-fitting clothes. There was a little bit of a swinging pendulum and I had to be told to stop wearing a Speedo. Just because you can doesn't mean you should.

If I had to choose one word that expressed my Foundational Value, it would be Integrity. Integrity is strength, truth, alignment, and fortitude. There is an unchangeable quality to your foundational values that makes them stalwart and strong, like the foundation of a house. When I was young, I had a lightness and lack of grounding that made having foundational values difficult. Joy and Love were strong for me when I was very young and these got replaced with fear, paranoia, and pain when I was using drugs. Today, I build my life on a foundation of integrity. My actions match up with my ideas, words, and thoughts. I am true to myself and consequently I am true to others. What do you hold as foundational for your life? What is the rest of Life built upon? Is it strong, consistent, and enduring? It is with these values and my Spiritual Center that I daily live my life to its fullest.

What lurks in the shadows of your life? What threatens your progress and eats you alive? I was always drawn to the story of "Little Red Riding Hood." I could never understand how it was that she could be so blind that the wolf was not her grandmother. The big teeth, the long nose, the foul smelling breath—or at least I assume it was foul. Actually, come to think of it, the foul breath might have

Chapter 10

been a characteristic of my grandmother. I think that it was because Red wanted it to be her grandmother. She expected it to be grandmother and was not even open to the possibility that it might be the dangerous wolf. This is the case for me with my addiction. This is why I stay vigilant.

This does not mean that I am in a constant state of fear about getting loaded or fat. I don't think that if I let my guard down for a second that addiction is going to take over my life. However, I am sensitive to the fact that I have used things outside myself to change the way I feel. I remember when I was writing my master's thesis and I was so insecure about the job that I was doing on it that I wanted to change the way I was feeling and I started smoking again. It didn't work. I was still feeling insecure about the work only now I stank like smoke. It took me another year and a half to quit smoking again. Even as I write this, I think that smoking would relax how I feel at this very moment—threat to progress. "Granny, what big teeth you have." It is not the big things that sneak up and scare me in the dark but the little things. Like the scariest things on earth are microscopic.

Spiritual truth is similar to a belief in God but differs slightly. If your belief in God is outside of yourself, your spiritual truth is within you and connects you to your Higher Self. I identify my spiritual truth with that which is my human connection with Spirit. I find that practices help in connecting with this truth include the practice of tithing. Tithing my time, talent, and treasure is the practice of taking 10 percent off the top to spend on my future.

I give myself to my recovery and spiritual communities through service and contribution of resources, and these communities will thrive for my benefit. Spiritual truth and tithing sounds wholly altruistic, but in reality, they are quite selfish. I want my life to be better so I give to that which makes my life better. Other people might benefit, but really, it is about me. Actually, how I treat others, how I show up in the world, and ultimately how the world shows up for me and to me is a direct reflection of the strength of my spiritual truth. When I care for my Spirit on the inside through practices on a regular basis then I am putting ritual at the center of my spirituality.

Several years ago, I was at a retreat and we were asked to craft our vision statement. If you have never done this, it can be a daunting task. I did not realize it at the time but I was being asked to dream. I was being given permission to dream and to open up to Spirit and allow my dreams into my waking consciousness. I don't remember what my actual statement was but it had to do with helping people recover from self-limiting beliefs and to do it on a grand scale. As much and as big as I saw myself in that vision I held on to the dream that if I helped just one person escape from a journey like I took, it would all be worth it.

In my life, I have lived so many of my dreams that I often stand in awe. I stand at the ready for the blessed sight of the next dream and I allow my dreams into my waking hours. It was a dream to write this book and to use it as a platform to help people transform their lives and that is what I am now doing. It is my dream to help that one small voice get bigger and that one dim light get brighter. What dreams do you have? What is the greatest wish for your life? If you want to journey into your Spirit and capture the vision of your dreams, I welcome you to try Rev. Michael Beckwith's *Life Visioning Process* CD series. Be prepared to see your future laid out before you and then get ready to take the next steps to get there.

Sorting through your dreams you will come across the one that comes up again and again. This, my loves, is no longer just a dream and has more of your attention. This is a goal. What dreams do you have that you want to become reality? What has your attention? I remember when I was practicing as a nurse I kept seeing a nurse practitioner whom I had seen while I was doing my nursing rotation. It seemed that every time I saw her something happened inside of me that brought the dream of being a nurse practitioner into my attention again. I began to nurture it and focus on what it would mean to be a nurse practitioner. I began to Craft my Goals.

Setting the Plan is the easy part. You have your G.I.F.T.S. and your goal. Now it just takes a bit of work to figure out the steps of getting to that goal. I find that working backwards from your goal is the most efficient way to plan, but that is easier said than done. I have what Benjamin Hoff in *The Tao of Pooh* describes as "Tigger Tendencies." This being said, planning is not a Tigger trait. I don't know how many times I have found myself lamenting that if I had just planned a bit better the process would have been easier. Sometimes I feel like a hiker who wants to go to some

Drugs, Food, Sex and *God*

wonderful lake in the mountains and drives to a trailhead and sets out hiking only to be featured on the five o'clock news with the headline "lost hiker." A map would have helped. This is what Setting the Plan is all about.

Finally, the step before you get to celebrate is Action. I love action. I talk about it all the time. "What are you going to DO about it," I have been known to badger. I wrote in my journal once, "Perhaps we should be called Human Doings because life is an active process." I am not going to participate in the whole doing-and-being argument today because they really are both necessary parts of living. What I know is that in order to change, you have to DO something different, and this book is about change. If I had been grounded in beingness then I would not have wound up in the mess that I had done to my life in the first place.

It takes action to go from being a good and wholesome kid to drugged-out degenerate; and it takes action to come back. I didn't wish myself into recovery, I worked at it. I did not hope myself employable, I changed. I did not pray myself into a relationship—oh wait, I did do that. Life is about action. Even inaction is an action unto itself.

Sometimes the smartest choice is nothing. I remember getting teased on the school bus as a kid. "Georgie Porgie pudding and pie, kissed the girls and made them cry," they taunted. Me, being so smart and mouthy, said, "Well the reason they cried is because I have such hot lips." Who says that? From then on I was "Hot Lips," a decidedly worse taunt. I learned a great deal from this experience and when I was beat up in prison for being a "fag" I decided the best

Chapter 10

course of action was nothing. I went to my cell to heal my bruises and my attacker went to the hole for a month. Who says we can't learn from our mistakes.

Action takes perseverance. Attaining a goal means walking on a long road at times, and taking no for an answer is almost like quitting. If I had taken no for an answer initially about the nurse practitioner program, I would be a Clinical Nurse Specialist now, wishing that I were a Nurse Practitioner. If I had quit when I wanted to, which was at the beginning of EVERY semester at Duke, I would not be a Doctor now, and this story would be incomplete. I prepared for the long term and long haul.

If I had been told on my first day in recovery that in fourteen years I would be a published author and I would be asked to speak about my journey in becoming a doctor, I would have sprayed latte foam out my nose in surprise. I am glad that Action happens slowly because there is preparation along the way. Thankfully, along the way, there are opportunities to stop and celebrate.

We get to Celebrate the big wins as well as the small successes. I remember getting my license reinstated to drive a car. It is remarkably difficult to get a license with Driving with License Suspended violations, unpaid traffic and parking tickets, and a felony record. That day was a celebration and I just wanted to drive, drive, drive. Then I bought a used truck and called my sponsor at the time to celebrate that success and goal attainment. It was steps like those that led me to walking across the stage at Duke University with a big blue puffy graduation cap, but thank God they didn't happen all at once.

I remember one night not long ago, I went to a graduation at the Rehabilitation Center of the Salvation Army or Sally Ann as it is so lovingly called. It was a celebration of completion and I was struck by how intentional that program is. A man I was sponsoring was graduating from the inpatient program. It was palpable how hard he had worked for the last six months to change his personal spiral direction. I never went to treatment, other than prison, so I had never thought about the encapsulation of the steps of intention that are present in a program like that.

Each of the five men who stood up to share their personal story told a little of my story. Each one of them started out with a glimpse of being steeped in struggle. Their stories were all different, like each of our stories are different, but I found the similarities striking.

One man said he had been sober for eighteen years and then went back to drinking. His wife was in the audience and there was a tangible feeling of joy and relief as he "testified" about his life. Sally Ann is profoundly a Christian organization and has a way that is so wonderfully accepting of the stories of these men and women finding their doors.

The struggles each of the men recounted had led them to the "bottom of the steps" of the building. This bottom was so allegorical and representative of the bottom that any of us can reach in our spiral downward. I watched and listened each describe the process of walking up the steps or taking the elevator as a way of surrender, physically surrendering their body, mind, and spirit to a very rich and full recovery program.

Chapter 10

The beneficiaries, as the residents are called, are given a set of beliefs if they come in without one. Being a Christian organization, the set is organized around the Christ figure or Christ story without the dogma of intolerance that is found in many of the strictest religious organizations. Incidentally, if you come in with your own set of beliefs you are encouraged to explore them deeply while you are there. The important thing is that you believe in something external until you are able to internalize it and believe in yourself and the power you have within. Some say it's the Christ, Buddha, Atman, or eternal presence within each of us.

In order to transition successfully in the program, beneficiaries do what is called an inventory, a fourth step. You take stock in your resentments, your feelings, your beliefs, and your assets in order for you to move out into the world. Then you are encouraged to live there, connected with the program while you set your dreams, goals, plans, and actions for a life full of celebration (and struggle).

But here I was sitting at a celebration. I know how the process of intentional living works, and each step is precious, methodical, and necessary. Leading up to this celebration was each of the steps after struggling up the stairs and surrendering to the program's set of beliefs.

I asked my friend how that process looked for him after taking his inventory. The dream he said was to complete the program and return to being an active and participating member of society. The goals were specifically laid out with the help of the program and his counselor.

Waiting the obligatory length of time and staying on track was the primary goal. Getting a sponsor to work with was also part of the goal setting as was writing out the fourth step inventory. The bigger dream of returning to society takes goal setting and planning of a different nature. He wrote out his resume and tailored it for the type of job that he had his heart set on. I helped him open up his dreams and find out what he was passionate about, deep down.

Planning out the resume and working with his counselor on his completion plan was all an essential part of his program. He would make lists of the things he needed to accomplish and then he checked them off as he took action.

Taking action was easy from this methodical and well thought-out plan. It is remarkable that a desperate, hopeless drug addict who had previously found himself suicidal without a future was walking across the stage in celebration of the completion of this set of steps and excited to be recognizing the struggle of the next set. I realized in that moment that his life and my life were not different at all.

I am so grateful that I have had the opportunity to live the life that I have lived thus far. I can't imagine living any other life. Today, I work in a career that I love. My joy is bringing beauty to people and rejuvenating their outward appearance to match their inward feeling. I eventually merged my business, Seattle Youthful, with the company I work for today, SkinSpirit. I love being Dr. George. Words do not do justice to what my life has become and I do hope that through this story I have given you a glimpse of what

Chapter 10

my life has been like. I know that if you struggle you can follow a defined set of steps to celebrate once again. I am with you on that path.

Best and blessed,

Dr. George

AFTERWORD

"One of the continuing miracles of recovery is becoming a productive, responsible member of society. We need to tread carefully into areas that expose us to ego-inflating experience, prestige, and manipulation that may be difficult for us. We have found that the way to remain a productive, responsible member of society is to put our recovery first."
Narcotics Anonymous,
Living Clean: The Journey Continues

Finally, I leave you with a fun poem that I wrote one day in the early 1990s. I wrote this on a napkin while I was sitting at the bar waiting for my dealer to show up. I do remember giggling with each line and know that even in the midst of my life I was having some spots of joy.

Words

Words that tumble off tongues; like tundra
Make many more maundered and muddled.

Like mire, perhaps, a word obsoleted
It looks as though something's deleted.

Like ad- or quag- although equally silly
The best place to admire a quagmire is hilly.

I think this could continue perchance
That is if you too like to dance.
With idioms or participles, dangling or no
Redundancies repeated again and again and on we go.

Drugs, Food, Sex and *God*

Alliterations are alright albeit
Take second chair to onomatopoeias.

Words that say what they are
Like drip, splash and twinkle
If you could hear from a star.

Is it better to be in a rut or milieu
Crack or crevasse
Revolution or coup.

Perception, perspective my word which word's right
The wrong word could possibly riot incite.

Or insight, good gravy, now context is key
I am still confused about "I" and "me."

If me thinks about the protestations of a maiden
And I am joined in my thinking
By my thinking friend, Hayden.

Then technically speaking although grammatically out of touch
Me and Hayden think the maiden doth protest too much.

An ending to this poem, don't you think, would prudent be
But an ending, how sad, it just is not me.

Instead of an ending, why not an ellipsis
Dot dot dot is how I would end this …

RESOURCES

Beckwith, Michael B. *Life Visioning: A Four-Stage Evolutionary Journey to Live as Divine Love*. Louisville, CO: CD Sounds True, Incorporated, 2008 (Audio CD)

Campbell, Joseph & Moyers, Bill. *The Power of Myth*. New York: Anchor Books, 1991.

Dispenza, Dr. Joe. *Breaking the Habit of Being Yourself*. Encephalon, LLC, 2014. (Audio CD)

Dyer, Wayne W. *The Power of Intention: Learning to Co-create Your World Your Way*. Carlsbad, CA: Hay House, 2010.

Henry, Dorinda G. *Bulldagger*. Amazon Digital Services, Inc., 2012. (ebook)

Hoff, Benjamin. *The Tao of Pooh*. Harmondsworth, Middlesex: Penguin Books, 1983.

Holmes, Ernest. *Science of Mind*. USA: Tarcher Putnam, 1938.

Koulouris, Melanie. Positive and Inspirational Quotes - Blog. *www.positiveandinspirationalquotes.blogspot.ca*

Narcotics Anonymous World Services, Inc. *Living Clean: The Journey Continues*. Van Nuys, CA: NA World Services, Inc., 2013.

Nicholson, Ester. *Soul Recovery – 12 Keys To Healing Addiction… and 12 Steps For The Rest of Us*. Agape Media International, LLC., 2013.

Singer, Michael. *The Untethered Soul: The Journey Beyond Yourself*. Oakland, CA: New Harbinger Publications, 2007.

Williamson, Marianne. *A Course in Weight Loss: 21 spiritual lessons for surrendering your weight forever.* Carlsbad, CA: Hay House, 2010.

AUTHOR BIOGRAPHY

Dr. George Baxter-Holder spent his childhood on Long Island, New York, and Vashon Island, Washington. He holds a Doctor of Nursing Practice from Duke University and a Masters in Nursing from the University of Washington. He started his own medical practice, which focuses on wellness and beauty and sold it to the company he works for now. During his very colourful life, Dr. George has battled drug and sex addiction, criminal convictions for drug dealing, obesity, the IRS, and a Mexican drug cartel. He has been in recovery from drug addiction for many years since serving time on a three-year sentence for drug possession. Today, he and his husband Travis live profoundly spiritual and intentional lives. Their only children are a tabby cat named Abigale and two beautiful Cavalier King Charles Spaniels, The Dollie Mama and Minnie Pearl.

Workshop and Keynote Speaker

Ask Dr. George to come and give an *Empowerment and Intentional Living* talk to your group, business or professional organization. Contact DrGeorge@GeorgeBaxter-Holder.com

SkinSpirit Skincare Clinic and Spa

If you are interested in wellness and beauty come and see Dr. George at SkinSpirit Skincare Clinic and Spa in Bellevue Square, Bellevue, WA.

Dr. George Baxter-Holder is a practicing Nurse Practitioner in the field of Facial Aesthetics. He specialized in the rejuvenation of 3D facial anatomy with the use of Dermal Fillers and Botox.

SkinSpirit
SKINCARE CLINIC AND SPA
2022 Bellevue Square
Bellevue, WA 98004
Website: www.SkinSpirit.com

Dr. George's Website:
www.GeorgeBaxter-Holder.com

Social Media:
Facebook:
www.facebook.com/pages/Drugs-Food-Sex-God/409278632524149
Twitter: www.twitter.com/DrugsFoodSexGod

If you want to get on the path to be a published author
with Influence Publishing please go to
www.InfluencePublishing.com

influence PUBLISHING

Inspiring books that influence change

More information on our other titles and how to submit
your own proposal can be found at
www.InfluencePublishing.com

CPSIA information can be obtained at www.ICGtesting.com
Printed in the USA
BVOW02s1632180515

400109BV00003B/6/P